Whillans's Tables

CW01084527

Finance Act 2008 Edition

Edited by

Mary Hyland
CA CTA (Fellow)

Kevin Walton
BA (Hons)

Members of the LexisNexis Group worldwide

United Kingdom	LexisNexis, a Division of Reed Elsevier (UK) Ltd, Halsbury House, 35 Chancery Lane, London, WC2A 1EL, and London House, 20-22 East London Street, Edinburgh EH7 4BQ
Australia	LexisNexis Butterworths, Chatswood, New South Wales
Austria	LexisNexis Verlag ARD Orac GmbH & Co KG, Vienna
Benelux	LexisNexis Benelux, Amsterdam
Canada	LexisNexis Canada, Markham, Ontario
China	LexisNexis China, Beijing and Shanghai
France	LexisNexis SA, Paris
Germany	LexisNexis Deutschland GmbH, Munster
Hong Kong	LexisNexis Hong Kong, Hong Kong
India	LexisNexis India, New Delhi
Italy	Giuffrè Editore, Milan
Japan	LexisNexis Japan, Tokyo
Malaysia	Malayan Law Journal Sdn Bhd, Kuala Lumpur
New Zealand	LexisNexis NZ Ltd, Wellington
Poland	Wydawnictwo Prawnicze LexisNexis Sp, Warsaw
Singapore	LexisNexis Singapore, Singapore
South Africa	LexisNexis Butterworths, Durban
USA	LexisNexis, Dayton, Ohio

First published in 1948

© Reed Elsevier (UK) Ltd 2008

Published by LexisNexis
This is a Tolley title

A CIP Catalogue record for this book is available from the British Library.

[Seventy-sixth edition]   ISBN for this volume 9781405729055

Typeset by Letterpart Ltd, Reigate, Surrey, UK

Printed in Italy by L.E.G.O. S.p.A. Lavis (TN)

Visit LexisNexis at www.lexisnexis.co.uk

Administration

Bank base rates

Period	Rate
from 10 April 2008	**5.00%**
7 February 2008–9 April 2008	5.25%
6 December 2007–6 February 2008	5.50%
5 July 2007–5 December 2007	5.75%
10 May 2007–4 July 2007	5.50%
11 January 2007–9 May 2007	5.25%
9 November 2006–10 January 2007	5.00%
3 August 2006–8 November 2006	4.75%
4 August 2005–2 August 2006	4.50%
5 August 2004–3 August 2005	4.75%
10 June 2004–4 August 2004	4.50%
6 May 2004–9 June 2004	4.25%
5 February 2004–5 May 2004	4.00%
6 November 2003–4 February 2004	3.75%
10 July 2003–5 November 2003	3.50%
6 February 2003–9 July 2003	3.75%
8 November 2001–5 February 2003	4.00%
4 October 2001–7 November 2001	4.50%
18 September 2001–3 October 2001	4.75%
2 August 2001–17 September 2001	5.00%
10 May 2001–1 August 2001	5.25%
5 April 2001–9 May 2001	5.50%
8 February 2001–4 April 2001	5.75%
10 February 2000–7 February 2001	6.00%
13 January 2000–9 February 2000	5.75%
4 November 1999–12 January 2000	5.50%
8 September 1999–3 November 1999	5.25%
10 June 1999–7 September 1999	5.00%
8 April 1999–9 June 1999	5.25%
4 February 1999–7 April 1999	5.50%
7 January 1999–3 February 1999	6.00%
10 December 1998–6 January 1999	6.25%
5 November 1998–9 December 1998	6.75%
8 October 1998–4 November 1998	7.25%
4 June 1998–7 October 1998	7.50%
6 November 1997–3 June 1998	7.25%
7 August 1997–5 November 1997	7.00%
10 July 1997–6 August 1997	6.75%
6 June 1997–9 July 1997	6.50%
6 May 1997–5 June 1997	6.25%
30 October 1996–5 May 1997	6.00%
6 June 1996–29 October 1996	5.75%
8 March 1996–5 June 1996	6.00%
19 January 1996–7 March 1996	6.25%

Due dates of tax

Capital gains tax

Normally 31 January following end of year of assessment. (TMA 1970 s 59B)
(See also *Extended due dates* under **Income tax**, below.)

Corporation tax

Generally
9 months and 1 day after end of accounting period. (FA 1998 Sch 19 para 29)
Instalments for larger companies (TMA 1970 s 59E, SI 1998/3175)
(A 'large company' is one whose taxable profits exceed £1.5m a year, divided by 1 plus the number of any active associated companies.)
    1st instalment: 6 months and 13 days from start of accounting period (or date of final instalment if earlier);
    2nd instalment: 3 months after 1st instalment, if length of accounting period allows;
    3rd instalment: 3 months after 2nd instalment, if length of accounting period allows;
    Final instalment: 3 months and 14 days from end of accounting period.
Transitional provisions percentage of total liability payable by instalments for accounting periods ending:
    after 30 June 1999 but before 1 July 2000: 60%
    after 30 June 2000 but before 1 July 2001: 72%
    after 30 June 2001 but before 1 July 2002: 88%
(balance due and payable in accordance with *Generally* above).
Close companies: tax on loans to participators
Loans etc made in accounting periods ending after 30 March 1996: 9 months and 1 day after the end of the accounting period. Previously 14 days after the end of the accounting period in which the loan was made. To be included in instalment payments for large companies (TMA 1970 s 59E(11), see above).

Income tax

Payments on account (TMA 1970 s 59A)
A payment on account is required where a taxpayer was assessed to income tax in the immediately preceding year to an amount exceeding the amount of tax deducted at source in respect of that year (subject to a de minimis limit, see below).
The payment on account is made in 2 equal instalments due on:
    (*a*) 31 January during the year of assessment, and
    (*b*) 31 July in the following year of assessment.
No payments on account are required where either:
    (*a*) the aggregate of the liability (including Class 4 NIC) for the preceding year (net of tax deducted at source) is less than £500; or
    (*b*) more than 80% of the taxpayer's income tax and Class 4 NIC liability for the preceding year was met by tax deducted at source (including PAYE).
Final payment (TMA 1970 s 59B, Sch 3ZA)
Balance of income tax due for a year of assessment (after deducting payments on account, tax deducted at source and credits in respect of dividends, etc) is due on:
31 January following end of year of assessment (TMA 1970 s 59B(4)).
Extended due dates:
    (*a*) If a taxpayer has given notice of liability within 6 months of the end of the year of assessment (under TMA 1970 s 7), but a notice to make a return is not given until after 31 October following the end of the year of assessment, the due date is 3 months after the notice is given (TMA 1970 s 59B(3)).
    (*b*) If tax is payable as a result of a taxpayer's notice of amendment, an HMRC notice of correction or an HMRC notice of closure following enquiry, in each case given less than 30 days before the due date (or the extended due date at (*a*) above), the due date is on or before the day following the end of a 30-day period beginning on the day on which the notice is given (TMA 1970 s 59B(5), Sch 3ZA).
    (*c*) If an assessment other than a self-assessment is made, tax payable under the assessment is due on the day following the end of a 30-day period beginning on the day on which notice of the assessment is given (TMA 1970 s 59B(6)).
The extensions under (*b*) and (*c*) do *not* alter the due date for *interest purposes* (see p 5).

Interest on overdue tax see p 5.
Remission of tax see p 7.
Repayment supplement see p 8.

Inheritance tax

Chargeable transfers other than on death, made between:

6 April and 30 September   –   30 April in next year.

1 October and 5 April   –   6 months after end of month in which chargeable transfer is made.

Chargeable events following conditional exemption for heritage etc property and charge on disposal of trees or underwood before the second death

                                   –   6 months after end of month in which chargeable event occurs.

Transfers on death

Earlier of   (*a*) 6 months after end of month in which death occurs, and

                         (*b*) delivery of account by personal representatives.

Tax or extra tax becoming payable on death:

(1)   chargeable transfers and potentially exempt transfers within 7 years of death, or

(2)   gifts in excess of £100,000 made to political parties before 15 March 1988 and within 1 year of death: due 6 months after end of month in which death takes place.

PAYE and national insurance

Employer's tax and Class 1 national insurance payable under PAYE.	19 April following deduction year (extended to 22 April where payments after 5 April 2004 are made by electronic means).
Class 1A national insurance.	19 July following year in which contributions due.
PAYE settlement agreement and Class 1B national insurance.	19 October following year to which agreement relates.
Class 4 national insurance.	See under income tax on p 4.

Stamp duties see p 90.

Interest on overdue tax

Interest runs from the due date (see p 4) to the date of payment, on the amount outstanding. For tax resulting from amendments/corrections to returns and from discovery assessments (under TMA 1970 s 29), interest normally runs from the annual filing date for the relevant tax year.
Interest is payable gross and is not tax deductible.

Income tax, capital gains tax, NICs Class 1, 1A, 4 and (from 6.4.99) 1B, and (from 1.10.99) stamp duty, SDRT and (from 26.9.05) stamp duty land tax

Period	Rate
from 6 January 2008	**7.5%**
6 August 2007–5 January 2008	8.5%
6 September 2006–5 August 2007	7.5%
6 September 2005–5 September 2006	6.5%
6 September 2004–5 September 2005	7.5%
6 December 2003–5 September 2004	6.5%
6 August 2003–5 December 2003	5.5%
6 November 2001–5 August 2003	6.5%
6 May 2001–5 November 2001	7.5%
6 February 2000–5 May 2001	8.5%
6 March 1999–5 February 2000	7.5%
6 January 1999–5 March 1999	8.5%
6 August 1997–5 January 1999	9.5%
31 January 1997–5 August 1997	8.5%

Surcharge on unpaid income tax and capital gains tax (TMA 1970 s 59C)

Where income tax or capital gains tax becomes payable and all or part of it remains unpaid the day following 28 days after the due date, the taxpayer is liable to a surcharge of 5% of the unpaid tax. A further surcharge of 5% is levied on any of the tax remaining unpaid six months and one day from the due date. Interest is payable on surcharge from the expiry of 30 days beginning on the day on which the surcharge is imposed until the date of payment chargeable at the above rate.

Corporation tax

Interest runs from the due date (see p 4) to the date of payment. For instalment payments by large companies for accounting periods ending after 30 June 1999, a special rate of interest runs from the due date to the earlier of the date of payment and nine months after the end of the accounting period (after which the normal rate applies).

Corporation tax self-assessment (accounting periods ending after 30 June 1999)

Period	Normal rate
from 6 January 2008	**7.5%**
6 August 2007–5 January 2008	8.5%
6 September 2006–5 August 2007	7.5%
6 September 2005–5 September 2006	6.5%
6 September 2004–5 September 2005	7.5%
6 December 2003–5 September 2004	6.5%
6 August 2003–5 December 2003	5.5%
6 November 2001–5 August 2003	6.5%

Period	Special rate for instalment payments (except where still unpaid nine months after end of accounting period)
from 21 April 2008	**6.00%**
18 February 2008–20 April 2008	6.25%
17 December 2007–17 February 2008	6.50%
16 July 2007–16 December 2007	6.75%
21 May 2007–15 July 2007	6.50%
22 January 2007–20 May 2007	6.25%
20 November 2006–21 January 2007	6.00%
14 August 2006–19 November 2006	5.75%
15 August 2005–13 August 2006	5.50%
16 August 2004–14 August 2005	5.75%
21 June 2004–15 August 2004	5.50%
17 May 2004–20 June 2004	5.25%
16 February 2004–16 May 2004	5.00%
17 November 2003–15 February 2004	4.75%
21 July 2003–16 November 2003	4.50%
17 February 2003–20 July 2003	4.75%
19 November 2001–16 February 2003	5.00%
15 October 2001–18 November 2001	5.50%
1 October 2001–14 October 2001	5.75%
13 August 2001–30 September 2001	6.00%
21 May 2001–12 August 2001	6.25%

Corporation tax pay and file (accounting periods ending after 30 September 1993)

Period	Rate
from 6 January 2008	**6.00%**
6 August 2007–5 January 2008	6.75%
6 September 2006–5 August 2007	6.00%
6 September 2005–5 September 2006	5.25%
6 September 2004–5 September 2005	6.00%
6 December 2003–5 September 2004	5.25%*
6 August 2003–5 December 2003	4.25%
6 November 2001–5 August 2003	5.00%

* This rate was corrected by HMRC (see news release HMRC 27/05 of 6 September 2005) and is higher than that previously used (5%). No attempt will be made to recover any further interest which may be due unless, exceptionally, a liability is reviewed.

Income tax on company payments (due on or after 14 October 1999)

Period	Rate
from 6 January 2008	**7.5%**
6 August 2007–5 January 2008	8.5%
6 September 2006–5 August 2007	7.5%
6 September 2005–5 September 2006	6.5%
6 September 2004–5 September 2005	7.5%
6 December 2003–5 September 2004	6.5%
6 August 2003–5 December 2003	5.5%
6 November 2001–5 August 2003	6.5%
6 May 2001–5 November 2001	7.5%
6 February 2000–5 May 2001	8.5%

Inheritance tax

Interest runs from the due date (see p 5) to the date of payment.

Period	Rate
from 6 January 2008	**4%**
6 August 2007–5 January 2008	5%
6 September 2006 to 5 August 2007	4%
6 September 2005–5 September 2006	3%
6 September 2004–5 September 2005	4%
6 December 2003–5 September 2004	3%
6 August 2003–5 December 2003	2%
6 November 2001–5 August 2003	3%
6 May 2001–5 November 2001	4%
6 February 2000–5 May 2001	5%
6 March 1999–5 February 2000	4%
6 October 1994–5 March 1999	5%
6 January 1994–5 October 1994	4%
6 December 1992–5 January 1994	5%
6 November 1992–5 December 1992	6%
6 July 1991–5 November 1992	8%
6 May 1991–5 July 1991	9%

Remission of tax

By concession, arrears of tax may be waived if they result from HMRC's failure to make proper and timely use of information supplied by the taxpayer or, where it affects the taxpayer's coding, by his or her employer. The concession also applies to information supplied by the Department for Work and Pensions affecting the taxpayer's entitlement to a retirement or widow's pension (see Concession A19). The concession only applies where the taxpayer could reasonably have believed that his or her affairs were in order and (unless the circumstances are exceptional) where the taxpayer is notified of the arrears more than 12 months after the end of the tax year in which HMRC received the information indicating that more tax was due.

Interest on overpaid tax

Income tax, capital gains tax, Class 1, 1A, 4 and (from 6.4.99) 1B national insurance contributions and (from 1.10.99) stamp duty and stamp duty reserve tax and (from 26.9.05) stamp duty land tax

Calculated as simple interest on the amount of tax repaid. The supplement is tax free.
See pp 9 and 10 for rates applicable to corporation tax and p 90 with respect to stamp duties.

Period	Rate
from 6 January 2008	**3.00%**
6 August 2007–5 January 2008	4.00%
6 September 2006–5 August 2007	3.00%
6 September 2005–5 September 2006	2.25%
6 September 2004–5 September 2005	3.00%*
6 December 2003–5 September 2004	2.25%*
6 August 2003–5 December 2003	1.50%*
6 November 2001–5 August 2003	2.25%*
6 May 2001–5 November 2001	3.00%*
6 February 2000–5 May 2001	4.00%
6 March 1999–5 February 2000	3.00%
6 January 1999–5 March 1999	4.00%
6 August 1997–5 January 1999	4.75%
6 February 1997–5 August 1997	4.00%
6 February 1996–5 February 1997	6.25%
6 March 1995–5 February 1996	7.00%
6 October 1994–5 March 1995	6.25%
6 January 1994–5 October 1994	5.50%
6 March 1993–5 January 1994	6.25%
6 December 1992–5 March 1993	7.00%
6 November 1992–5 December 1992	7.75%
6 October 1991–5 November 1992	9.25%
6 July 1991–5 October 1991	10.00%
6 May 1991–5 July 1991	10.75%
6 March 1991–5 May 1991	11.50%

* These rates were corrected by HMRC (see news release HMRC 27/05 of 6 September 2005) and are lower than those previously used. No attempt will be made to recover amounts overpaid by HMRC unless, exceptionally, a repayment is reviewed.

Income tax

(TA 1988 s 824; FA 1997 s 92; ITTOIA 2005 s 749)
From 1996–97 (1997–98 for partnerships whose trade, profession or business commenced before 6 April 1994) repayment supplement applies to:
- (a) amounts paid on account of income tax
- (b) income tax paid by or on behalf of an individual
- (c) surcharges on late payments of tax
- (d) penalties incurred by an individual under any provision of TMA 1970

but excluding amounts paid in excess of the maximum the taxpayer is required to pay.
Except for tax deducted at source, the repayment supplement runs *from* the date on which the tax, penalty or surcharge was paid *to* the date on which the order for repayment is issued. For tax deducted at source, repayment supplement runs from 31 January after the end of the tax year for which the tax was deducted.

Capital gains tax

(TCGA 1992 s 283; FA 1997 s 92)
From 1996–97 repayment supplement runs *from* the date on which the tax was paid *to* the date on which the order for repayment is issued.

Inheritance tax

(IHTA 1984 s 235)
Repayments of inheritance tax or interest paid carries interest *from* the date of payment *to* the date on which the order for repayment is issued. The prescribed rates for unpaid tax apply equally to repayment supplements – see p 7.

Companies

Corporation tax self-assessment (accounting periods ending after 30 June 1999)

Normal rates

Rates on overpaid corporation tax in respect of periods after normal due date (SI 1989/1297 reg 3BB):

Period	Rate
from 6 January 2008	**4%**
6 August 2007–5 January 2008	5%
6 September 2006–5 August 2007	4%
6 September 2005–5 September 2006	3%
6 September 2004–5 September 2005	4%
6 December 2003–5 September 2004	3%
6 August 2003–5 December 2003	2%
6 November 2001–5 August 2003	3%
6 May 2001–5 November 2001	4%
6 February 2000–5 May 2001	5%

Special rates

For instalment payments by large companies and early payments by other companies, a special rate of interest runs from the date the excess arises (but not earlier than the due date of the first instalment) to the earlier of the date the repayment order is issued and nine months after the end of the accounting period after which the normal rate of interest (as above) applies.

Rates on overpaid instalment payments and on corporation tax paid early (but not due by instalments):

Period	Rate
from 21 April 2008	**4.75%**
18 February 2008–20 April 2008	5.00%
17 December 2007–17 February 2008	5.25%
16 July 2006-16 December 2007	5.50%
21 May 2007–15 July 2007	5.25%
22 January 2007–20 May 2007	5.00%
20 November 2006–21 January 2007	4.75%
14 August 2006–19 November 2006	4.50%
15 August 2005–13 August 2006	4.25%
16 August 2004–14 August 2005	4.50%
21 June 2004–15 August 2004	4.25%
17 May 2004–20 June 2004	4.00%
16 February 2004–16 May 2004	3.75%
17 November 2003–15 February 2004	3.50%
21 July 2003–16 November 2003	3.25%
17 February 2003–20 July 2003	3.50%
19 November 2001–16 February 2003	3.75%
15 October 2001–18 November 2001	4.25%
1 October 2001–14 October 2001	4.50%
13 August 2001–30 September 2001	4.75%
21 May 2001–12 August 2001	5.00%
16 April 2001–20 May 2001	5.25%
19 February 2001–15 April 2001	5.50%
21 February 2000–18 February 2001	5.75%
24 January 2000–20 February 2000	5.50%
15 November 1999–23 January 2000	5.25%
20 September 1999–14 November 1999	5.00%
21 June 1999–19 September 1999	4.75%
19 April 1999–20 June 1999	5.00%

Corporation tax pay and file (accounting periods ending before 1 July 1999)

Repayments of corporation tax, repayments of income tax in respect of payments received, payments of tax credits in respect of franked investment income received, and (before its abolition from 6 April 1999) repayments of ACT in respect of foreign income dividends made after the material date. (FA 1998 ss 31, 32, SI 1999/358.)

Calculated *from* the material date *to* the date the repayment order is issued.

For corporation tax, the material date is the later of:

(*a*) the date on which the tax was paid; and

(*b*) the date on which the tax became, or would have become, due and payable – generally, nine months and one day after the end of the accounting period.

(For ACT, the material date was the date on which corporation tax for the accounting period in which the distribution was made became, or would have become, due and payable – generally, nine months and one day after the end of the accounting period.)

For repayments of income tax in respect of payments received and payments of tax credits in respect of franked investment income received, the material date is the date on which corporation tax for the accounting period in which the payments or the franked investment income were received became, or would have become, due and payable. Again, this is generally nine months and one day after the end of the accounting period.

Where there is in any accounting period ('the later period') a non-trading deficit on a company's loan relationships and a claim is made to carry this deficit back to an earlier accounting period ('the earlier period'), then interest on any repayment of corporation tax for the earlier period (or of income tax on a payment received in the earlier period) resulting from the claim begins to run only after the date on which the corporation tax for the *later* period (the period in which the non-trading deficit arose) became due and payable. (TA 1988 s 826(7C).)

A similar rule (s 826(7) repealed for accounting periods beginning on or after 6 April 1999) applied to the carry-back of surplus ACT as applies to the carry-back of a non-trading deficit.

Trading losses carried back for more than 12 months (s 826(7A), (7B))

Where a claim is made under TA 1988 s 393A(1) to set off a loss incurred in a later period against the profits of an earlier period not falling within the 12 months immediately preceding the later period, and

(*a*) a repayment of corporation tax in respect of that earlier period or a repayment of income tax in respect of a payment received in the earlier period; or

(*b*) following a claim under TA 1988 s 242 to include surplus franked investment income in profits available for set-off, a payment of the whole or part of the tax credit comprised in franked investment income of the earlier period,

is made, interest in respect of that part of the repayment due to the claim under TA 1988 s 393A(1) or TA 1988 s 242 (so far as it relates to the claim under s 393A(1)) begins to run only after the date on which the corporation tax in respect of the later period (the lossmaking period) became, or would have become, due and payable.

Period	Rate
from 6 January 2008	**2.75%**
6 August 2007–5 January 2008	3.5%
6 September 2006–5 August 2007	2.75%
6 September 2005–5 September 2006	2.00%
6 September 2004–5 September 2005	2.75%
6 December 2003–5 September 2004	2.00%
6 August 2003–5 December 2003	1.25%
6 November 2001–5 August 2003	2.00%
6 May 2001–5 November 2001	2.75%
6 February 2000–5 May 2001	3.50%
6 March 1999–5 February 2000	2.75%
6 January 1999–5 March 1999	3.25%
6 August 1997–5 January 1999	4.00%

Certificates of tax deposit

The Series 7 Prospectus came into operation on 1 October 1993. Certificates are not available for purchase for use against corporation tax liabilities. Certificates are available to individuals, trustees, companies or other persons or bodies for the payment of any taxes or other liabilities listed in the schedule to the Prospectus. Minimum first deposit £2,000; subsequent deposits not less than £500. Interest is paid gross and is chargeable to tax. It will only be paid for the first six years of a deposit. A deposit bears interest for the first year at the rate in force at the time of the deposit and for each subsequent year at the rate in force on the anniversary of the deposit.

Date	Amount	Held for (mths in yr)	Pay't of tax %	Cashed %
11.6.04–5.8.04	Under £100,000	no limit	1.00	0.50
	£100,000 or over	under 1	1.00	0.50
		1–under 3	3.75	1.75
		3–under 6	3.50	1.75
		6–12	3.75	1.75
6.8.04–4.8.05	Under £100,000	no limit	1.25	0.50
	£100,000 or over	under 1	1.25	0.50
		1–12	3.75	1.75
5.8.05–3.8.06	Under £100,000	no limit	1.00	0.50
	£100,000 or over	under 1	1.00	0.50
		1–under 3	3.50	1.75
		3–under 6	3.25	1.50
		6–12	3.00	1.50
4.8.06–9.11.06	Under £100,000	no limit	1.75	0.75
	£100,000 or over	under 1	1.75	0.75
		1–under 3	4.25	2.00
		3–under 6	4.25	2.00
		6–12	4.00	2.00
10.11.06–11.1.07	Under £100,000	no limit	1.50	0.75
	£100,000 or over	under 1	1.50	0.75
		1–under 3	4.00	2.00
		3–under 6	4.00	2.00
		6–12	3.75	1.75
12.1.07–10.5.07	Under £100,000	no limit	1.50	0.75
	£100,000 or over	under 1	1.50	0.75
		1–under 3	4.25	2.00
		3–under 6	4.00	2.00
		6–12	4.00	2.00
11.5.07–5.7.07	Under £100,000	no limit	2.00	1.00
	£100,000 or over	under 1	2.00	1.00
		1–under 3	4.75	2.25
		3–under 6	4.50	2.25
		6–12	4.50	2.25
6.7.07–6.12.07	Under £100,000	no limit	2.25	1.10
	£100,000 or over	under 1	2.25	1.10
		1–under 3	5.00	2.50
		3–under 6	4.75	2.25
		6–12	4.75	2.25
7.12.07–7.02.08	Under £100,000	no limit	3.00	1.50
	£100,000 or over	under 1	3.00	1.50
		1–under 3	5.50	2.75
		3–under 6	5.00	2.50
		6–9	4.75	2.25
		9–12	4.50	2.25
8.02.08–10.04.08	Under £100,000	no limit	2.00	1.00
	£100,000 or over	under 1	2.00	1.00
		1–under 3	4.50	2.25
		3–under 6	4.25	2.00
		6–under 9	4.00	2.00
		9–12	3.75	1.50
11.04.08–	**Under £100,000**	**No limit**	**2.00**	**1.00**
	£100,000 or over	**under 1**	**2.00**	**1.00**
		1–under 3	**4.75**	**2.25**
		3–under 6	**4.50**	**2.25**
		6–under 9	**4.25**	**2.00**
		9–12	**4.25**	**2.00**

Penalties

Personal tax and corporation tax

Offence	Penalty
Failure to notify chargeability to income or capital gains tax within six months of tax year or to corporation tax within one year of accounting period (TMA 1970 s 7; FA 1998 Sch 18 para 2).	Up to tax liability still unpaid after 31 January following tax year (IT or CGT) or one year after end of accounting period (CT).
Failure to render return for income tax or capital gains tax (TMA 1970 ss 93, 93A).	(*a*) Initial penalty of £100 (or tax due if less);
	(*b*) upon direction by Commissioners, further penalty up to £60 for each day failure continues;
	(*c*) if failure continues after six months from filing date, and no penalty imposed under (*b*), a further penalty of £100 (or tax due if less);
	(*d*) if failure continues after one year from filing date, a further penalty up to amount of tax due.
Failure to render return for corporation tax (FA 1998 Sch 18 paras 17, 18).	(*a*) £100 if up to three months late (£500 if previous two returns also late);
	(*b*) £200 if over three months late (£1,000 if previous two returns also late);
	(*c*) if failure continues on final day for delivery of return or, if later, 18 months after return period, 10% of tax unpaid 18 months after return period (20% of tax unpaid at that date if return not made within two years of return period).
Failure to maintain records (TMA 1970 s 12B).	Up to £3,000.
Fraudulently or negligently making an incorrect statement in connection with a claim to reduce payments on account (TMA 1970 s 59A).	Up to the amount (or additional amount) payable on account if a correct statement had been made.
Fraudulently or negligently delivering incorrect return or accounts or making an incorrect claim for an allowance, deduction or relief (TMA 1970 ss 95, 95A; FA 1998 Sch 18 para 89).	Up to amount of tax underpaid by reason of incorrectness for (IT and CGT) the tax year (or following tax year and any preceding tax year) in which the return or claim is delivered, (CT) the accounting period(s) to which the return or claim relates.
Failure to remedy error discovered on an incorrect corporation tax return without unreasonable delay.	Up to amount of tax underpaid by reason of incorrectness for the accounting period to which the return or claim relates.
Failure to notify within charge to corporation tax within three months after the beginning of the first accounting period and any subsequent accounting period not following on immediately from the end of a previous accounting period. With effect for accounting periods beginning on or after 22 July 2004 (FA 2004 s 55).	(*a*) Initial penalty up to £300; and
	(*b*) a continuing penalty up to £60 for each day on which the failure continues.
Failure to register as self-employed (and liable to Class 2 NIC) within three months after month in which self-employment begins (SI 2001/1004 reg 87).	Up to £100.

PAYE returns

Offence	Penalty
Failure to submit return P9D or P11D (benefits in kind) by due date (6 July following subsequent tax years) (TMA 1970 s 98(1)).	(*a*) Initial penalty up to £300; and (*b*) continuing penalty up to £60 for each day on which the failure continues.
Fraudulently or negligently submitting incorrect return P9D or P11D (TMA 1970 s 98(2)).	Penalty up to £3,000.
Failure to submit returns P14 (individual end of year summary), P35 (annual return), P38 or P38A (supplementary returns for employees not on P35) by due date (19 May following tax year) (TMA 1970 s 98A).	(*a*) First 12 months: penalty of £100 for each 50 employees (or part thereof) for each month the failure continues; (*b*) failures exceeding 12 months: penalty up to amount of PAYE or NIC due and unpaid after 19 April following tax year.
Fraudulently or negligently submitting incorrect forms P14, P35, P38 or P38A (TMA 1970 s 98A).	Penalty up to the amount of tax due.

Offence	Penalty
Failure to submit returns P11D(b) (Class 1A NIC returns) by due date (19 July following tax year, extended for 2000/01 only to 19 September 2001) (SI 2001/1004 reg 81).	(*a*) First 12 months: penalty of £100 for each 50 employees (or part thereof) for each month the failure continues (but total penalty not to exceed total Class 1A NIC due); (*b*) failures exceeding 12 months: a penalty not exceeding the amount of Class 1A NIC due and unpaid after 19 July following tax year.
Failure to submit information in connection with mandatory e-filing from 2004/05 onwards (SI 1993/744 as amended).	Penalty based on number of employees not exceeding £3,000 for 1,000 or more employees.

Inheritance tax returns and information

Offence	Penalty
Failure to deliver an account within 12 months of death (unless tax is less than £100 or there is a reasonable excuse) (IHTA 1984 s 245).	(*a*) Initial penalty of (up to) £100 (or the amount of tax payable if less); (*b*) further penalty up to £60 (where penalty determined by court or Special Commissioners) for each day on which the failure continues;
1 The fixed penalty in (*a*) and (*c*) relates to failures where the account is due by 22 January 2005 (FA 2004 s 295(5)).	(*c*) if failure continues after six months after the date on which account is due, and proceedings not commenced, a further penalty of (up to) £100 (or amount of tax payable if less); and
2 Where the account is due on or before 22 July 2004, the penalty in (*d*) relates to failures continuing after 21 July 2005 (FA 2004 s 295(6)).	(*d*) if failure continues one year after end of the period in which account is due (where the account is due after 22 July 2004)[2], and IHT is payable, a penalty not exceeding £3,000.
Failure to submit account or notify HMRC under IHTA 1984 s 218A if a disposition on a death is varied within six months of the variation and additional tax is payable (IHTA 1984 s 245A(1A), (1B)).	(*a*) Initial penalty up to £100; (*b*) further penalty up to £60 (if determined by court or Special Commissioners) for each day on which the failure continues; (*c*) up to £3,000 if failure continues after 12 months from date notification is due (where account due after 22 July 2004).
Failure to provide documents etc under IHTA 1984 s 219A(1) or (4) (IHTA 1984 s 245A(3)).	(*a*) Initial penalty up to £50; and (*b*) further penalty up to £30 (where penalty determined by court or Special Commissioners) for each day on which the failure continues.
Taxpayer fraudulently or negligently delivering, furnishing or producing incorrect accounts, information or documents (IHTA 1984 s 247; FA 2004 s 295(4), (9)).	(Accounts etc delivered after 22 July 2004) penalty up to the amount of tax payable. (Accounts etc delivered on or before 22 July 2004) (*a*) in the case of fraud, penalty up to aggregate of £3,000 and the amount payable; and (*b*) in the case of negligence, penalty up to the aggregate of £1,500 and the amount of tax payable.
Person other than the taxpayer fraudulently or negligently delivering, furnishing or producing incorrect accounts, information or documents (IHTA 1984 s 247(3); FA 2004 s 295(4), (9)).	(Accounts etc delivered after 22 July 2004) penalty up to £3,000. (Accounts etc delivered on or before 22 July 2004) (*a*) in the case of fraud, penalty up to £3,000; and (*b*) in the case of negligence, penalty up to £1,500.
Incorrect return etc: Assisting in or inducing the delivery, furnishing or production of any account, information or document knowing it to be incorrect (IHTA 1984 s 247(4)).	Up to £3,000.

Special returns of information

Offence	Penalty
Failure to comply with a notice to deliver a return or other document, furnish particulars or make anything available for inspection under any of the provisions listed in column 1 of the table in TMA 1970 s 98.	(a) Initial penalty up to £300 (£3,000 in relation to TA 1988 s 765A (movements of capital between residents of EU Member States); (b) further penalty up to £60 (£600) for each day on which the failure continues.
Failure to furnish information, give certificates or produce documents or records under any of the provisions listed in column 2 of the table in TMA 1970 s 98.	(a) Initial penalty up to £300; and (b) further penalty up to £60 for each day on which the failure continues.
Fraudulently or negligently delivering any incorrect document, information etc required under the above provisions.	Penalty up to £3,000.
Failure to deduct income tax at source from payments of interest or royalties under TA 1988 ss 349(1), 350(1) where the exemption does not apply and the company did not believe or could not reasonably have believed that it would apply (TMA 1970 s 98(4A)–(4D)).	(a) Initial penalty up to £3,000; and (b) further penalty up to £600 for each day on which the failure continues.
Advance pricing agreements: Fraudulently or negligently making a false or misleading statement in the preparation of, or application to enter into, any advance pricing agreement (FA 1999 s 86).	Penalty up to £10,000.
Declaration of non-UK residence: Fraudulently or negligently making a false or misleading declaration of non-UK residence to a deposit-taker or building society under ITA 2007 ss 858-861 (TMA 1970 s 99B).	Penalty up to £3,000.

Other offences by taxpayers, agents etc

Offence	Penalty
Falsification of documents. Intentionally falsifying, concealing or destroying documents required under TMA 1970 ss 20, 20A or 20BA (TMA 1970 s 20BB).	On summary conviction, a fine up to the statutory maximum (£5,000); on conviction on indictment, imprisonment for a term not exceeding two years or a fine or both.
Failure to produce documents etc for the purposes of an enquiry under TMA 1970 s 19A or under FA 1998 Sch 18 para 27 (TMA 1970 s 97AA; FA 1998 Sch 18 para 29).	(a) Initial penalty of £50; and (b) further penalty up to £30 (if determined by HMRC) or £150 (if determined by Commissioners) for each day on which failure continues.
European Economic Interest Groupings– Offences in connection with the supply of information: (i) failure to supply information	Initial penalty up to £300 per member of the Grouping at the time of failure and after direction by the Commissioners: continuing penalty up to £60 per member of the Grouping at the end of the day for each day on which the failure continues.
(ii) fraudulent or negligent delivery of an incorrect return, accounts or statement (TMA 1970 s 98B).	Up to £3,000 for each member of the Grouping at the time of delivery.
Assisting in the delivery of incorrect returns, accounts or information (TMA 1970 s 99).	Penalty up to £3,000.
Certificates of non-liability to income tax: Fraudulently or negligently giving such a certificate for the purposes of receiving interest gross on a bank or building society account, or failing to comply with an undertaking given in such a certificate (TMA 1970 s 99A).	Penalty up to £3,000.
Refusal to allow a deduction of income tax at source (TMA 1970 s 106).	£50.
Obstruction of officer in inspection of property to ascertain its market value (TMA 1970 s 111).	Up to £50.
Construction Industry Scheme: (pre 1 April 2007 scheme) Failure by contractor to check validity of registration card (TA 1988 s 566(2B)–(2E)).	Up to £3,000.
(pre 1 April 2007 scheme) Fraudulent attempt by sub-contractor to obtain or misuse a sub-contractor's certificate (TA 1988 s 561(10), (11)).	Up to £3,000.
Construction Industry Scheme: (post 31 March 2007 scheme) Making false statements etc for the purpose of obtaining a gross payment certificate (FA 2004 s 72).	Up to £3,000.

Offence	Penalty
Witnesses before Commissioners: Neglect or refusal to appear before Commissioners or refusal to be sworn or answer questions (SI 1994/1812).	Up to £1,000.
Fraudulent evasion of income tax (FA 2000 s 144).	On summary conviction, imprisonment for up to six months or a fine up to the statutory maximum (£5,000); on conviction on indictment, imprisonment for up to seven years or a fine or both.
Enterprise investment scheme relief: Issue by a company of a certificate of approval for such relief fraudulently or negligently or without the authority of HMRC (TA 1988 s 306(6)).	Not exceeding £3,000.
Treasury consent: Creation or transfer of shares or debentures in a non-resident subsidiary company without the consent of HM Treasury (TA 1988 s 766).	On conviction on indictment— (*a*) imprisonment for not more than two years or a fine, or both; or (*b*) in the case of a UK company, a fine not exceeding the greater of £10,000, or three times the tax payable by the company attributable to income and gains arising in the previous 36 months.
Deliberately or recklessly failing to pay corporation tax due in respect of total liability of company for accounting period, or fraudulently or negligently making claim for repayment (TMA 1970 s 59E(4); SI 1998/3175 reg 13).	Penalty not exceeding twice amount of interest charged under SI 1998/3175 reg 7.
Failure of a company to maintain records (other than those only required for claims, etc, or dividend vouchers and certificates of income tax deducted where other evidence is available) (FA 1998 Sch 18 para 23).	Penalty not exceeding £3,000.
Failure to notify notifiable proposals or notifiable arrangements, or failure to notify the client of the relevant scheme reference number under the provisions of FA 2004 ss 308(1), (3), 309(1), 310 or s 312(1).	(*a*) An initial penalty not exceeding £5,000; (*b*) a continuing penalty not exceeding £600 for each day on which the failure continues after imposition of initial penalty.

Failure to notify scheme reference number etc under FA 2004 s 313(1);
  for second failure, occurring within three years from the date on which the first failure began;
  for subsequent failures, occurring within three years from the date on which the previous failure began.
[TMA 1970 s 98C; FA 2004 s 315(1)].
	Penalty of £100 in respect of each scheme to which the failure relates;
	  penalty of £500 in respect of each scheme to which the failure relates;
	  penalty of £1,000 in respect of each scheme to which the failure relates.

Mitigation of penalties

HMRC have discretion to mitigate or entirely remit any penalty or to stay or compound any penalty proceedings (TMA 1970 s 102).

Interest on penalties

Penalties under TMA 1970 Parts II (ss 7–12B), IV (ss 28A–43B), VA (ss 59A–59D) and X (ss 93–107) carry interest at the prescribed rate (see p 14): TMA 1970 s 103A. Surcharges on unpaid income tax and capital gains tax carry interest under TMA 1970 s 59C.

FA 2007 and FA 2008 provisions regarding penalties

For returns for periods commencing on or after 1 April 2008 and where the return is due on or after 1 April 2009, a new penalty regime is introduced for IT, CT, CGT, PAYE, CIS and VAT. Penalties are determined as a percentage of potential lost revenue. The percentage to be applied is determined according to whether the inaccuracy giving rise to the penalty was 'careless' (up to 30%) 'deliberate but not concealed' (up to 70%) or 'deliberate and concealed' (up to 100%). FA 2008 extends the regime to penalties for failure to notify chargeability and where a third party deliberately supplies false information, or withholds information, leading another person to submit an inaccurate return or document. These provisions will take effect on a date to be appointed.

Time limits for claims and elections

Whenever possible, a claim or election must be made on the tax return or by an amendment to the return (TMA 1970 s 42 and FA 1998 Sch 18 paras 9, 10, 67 and 79). Exceptions to this general rule are dealt with in TMA 1970 Sch 1A. Except where another period is expressly prescribed, a claim for relief in respect of income tax and capital gains tax must be made within five years from the 31 January following the year of assessment to which it relates. From a date to be appointed, the time limit is to be changed to four years after the end of the tax year. (TMA 1970 s 43(1); FA 2008 Sch 39 para 12). The time limit for claims by companies remains at is six years until a date to be appointed when it will reduce to four years from the end of the accounting period to which it relates (TMA 1970 s 43(1)(43(1)(*b*)) and, for accounting periods ending after 1 July 1999, FA 1998 Sch 18 para 55 and FA 2008 Sch 39 para 44).

The tables below set out some of the main exceptions to the general limits.

Changes in time limits for claims and assessments are to be introduced from a date to be determined.

Income tax

Claim	Time limit
Trading losses: Loss sustained in a trade, profession or vocation to be set against other income of the year or the last preceding year. Extended to certain pre-trading expenditure by TA 1988 s 401 and ITTOIA 2005 s 57 (ITA 2007 s 64).	One year after 31 January next following tax year in which loss arose.
Unrelieved trading losses to be set against capital gains (TCGA 1992 ss 261B, 261C).	One year after 31 January next following tax year in which loss sustained.
Losses of new trade etc: Loss sustained in the first four years of a new trade, profession or vocation to be offset against other income arising in the three years immediately preceding the year of loss. Extended to certain pre-trading expenditure by TA 1988 s 401 and ITTOIA 2005 s 57 (ITA 2007 s 72).	One year after 31 January next following tax year in which loss sustained.
Property business losses: Claim for relief against total income (ITA 2007 s 124).	One year after 31 January next following tax year.
Loss on disposal of unlisted shares: Loss on disposal of shares in an EIS company or a qualifying trading company to be offset against other income of the year of loss or the last preceding year (ITA 2007 s 124).	One year after 31 January next following tax year in which loss incurred.
Gift aid: Election to treat donations to charity under gift aid made after 5 April 2003 as made in the previous tax year (ITA 2007 s 426).	On or before date on which donor delivers tax return for the previous tax year and not later than 31 January after that year.

Capital gains

Claim	Time limit
Assets of negligible value: Loss to be allowed where the value of an asset has become negligible (TCGA 1992 s 24(2)).	Two years after end of chargeable period of deemed sale (and reacquisition).
Assets held on 31 March 1982: Events occurring prior to 31 March 1982 to be ignored in computing gains arising after 5 April 1988 (TCGA 1992 s 35(5), (6) as amended).	One year after 31 January next following tax year in which first relevant disposal made after 5.4.88 (capital gains tax); two years after end of accounting period in which first relevant disposal made after 31.3.88 (corporation tax).
Main residence: Determination of main residence for principal private residence exemption (TCGA 1992 s 222(5)(*a*)).	Two years after acquisition of second residence.
Relief for loans to traders: Losses on certain loans to traders to be allowed as capital losses (TCGA 1992 s 253(3)).	Two years.
Relief for loans to traders (payments by guarantor): Losses arising from payments by guarantor of certain irrecoverable loans to traders to be allowed as capital losses at time of claim or 'earlier time' (TCGA 1992 s 253(4), (4A); FA 1996 s 135(2)).	Five years after 31 January following tax year in which payment made (capital gains tax); six years after end of accounting period in which payment made (corporation tax). These time limits to be changed, from a date to be appointed, to four years after the end of the tax year in each case.
Election for valuation at 6 April 1965: Gain on a disposal of an asset held at 6 April 1965 to be computed as if the asset had been acquired on that date. An election once made is irrevocable (TCGA 1992 Sch 2 para 17).	One year after 31 January following tax year in which disposal made (capital gains tax); two years after end of accounting period in which disposal made (corporation tax); or such further time as HMRC may allow.

Corporation tax

Claim	Time limit
Trading losses: Loss sustained by a company in a trade in an accounting period to be offset against profits of that accounting period and profits of the preceding year. Extended to certain pre-trading expenditure by TA 1988 s 401 (TA 1988 s 393A(1), (2A), (10)).	Two years or such further period as HMRC may allow.
Group relief: Group relief to be given for accounting periods ending after 30 June 1999. The surrendering company must consent to the claim (FA 1998 Sch 18 paras 66–77).	The last of: (*a*) one year from filing date of claimant company's return for accounting period for which claim is made; (*b*) 30 days after end of an enquiry into return; (*c*) if HMRC amend return after an enquiry, 30 days after issue of notice of amendment; (*d*) if an appeal is made against amendment, 30 days after determination of appeal; (or such later time as HMRC may allow).
Non-trading deficit on loan relationship: Claim for non-trading deficits on loan relationships (including non-trading debits on derivative contracts) in an accounting period ending after 30 September 2002 to be:	
(*a*) offset against profits of same period or carried back (FA 1996 s 83, Sch 8 paras 1, 3);	Two years after end of accounting period in which deficit arose (or such later time as HMRC may allow).
(*b*) treated as non-trading deficit of subsequent accounting period to be carried forward to succeeding accounting periods (FA 1996 s 83, Sch 8).	Two years after end of that subsequent accounting period.
Intangible assets: Election to replace accounts depreciation with fixed writing-down allowance of 4% (FA 2002 Sch 29 para 10).	Two years after end of the accounting period in which asset was created or acquired.
Research and development: Claim for tax relief to be made, amended or withdrawn in company tax return (or amended return) (FA 1998 Sch 18 paras 83E, 83LE).	One year from the filing date for return or such later time as HMRC may allow.
UITF 40 spreading adjustment: Election to treat it as arising and charged in an accounting period rather than spreading it over three to six years (FA 2006, Sch 15 para 13).	One year from filing date for return.

Capital allowances

Claim	Time limit
Corporation tax claims (accounting periods ending after 30 June 1999): Claims, amended claims and withdrawals of claims in respect of corporation tax capital allowances for accounting periods ending after 30 June 1999 (CAA 2001 s 3(2), (3)(*b*), FA 1998 Sch 18 para 82).	The last of: (*a*) one year after filing date of claimant company's return for accounting period for which claim is made; (*b*) 30 days after end of enquiry into return; (*c*) if HMRC amend the return after an enquiry, 30 days after issue of notice of amendment; (*d*) if appeal is made against amendment, 30 days after determination of appeal; (or such later time as HMRC may allow).
Short life assets: Plant or machinery to be treated as a short life asset (CAA 2001 s 85(2)).	One year after 31 January after tax year in which chargeable period ends (IT); two years after end of chargeable period (CT).
Connected persons: Succession to a trade between connected persons to be ignored in computing capital allowances (CAA 2001 s 266).	Two years after date of the succession.
Sales between persons under common control treated as made at the lower of open market value and tax written down value (CAA 2001 s 570(5)).	Two years after date of the disposal.

Exchanges

Recognised stock exchanges

The following is a list of countries with exchanges which have been designated as recognised stock exchanges under TA 1988 s 841. Unless otherwise specified, any stock exchange (or options exchange) in a country listed below is a recognised stock exchange for the purposes of ITA 2007 s 1005 and TA 1988 s 841, provided it is recognised under the law of the country concerned relating to stock exchanges.

An amended definition of 'recognised stock exchange' is substituted by FA 2007 s 109, Sch 26. HMRC may make an order designating a market in the UK as a recognised stock exchange.

Country	Date of recognition
Australian Stock Exchange and its stock exchange subsidiaries	22 September 1988
Austria[3]	22 October 1970
Belgium[3]	22 October 1970
Bermuda	4 December 2007
Brazil	
Rio De Janeiro Stock Exchange	17 August 1995
São Paulo Stock Exchange	11 December 1995
Canada	
Any stock exchange prescribed for the purposes of the Canadian Income Tax Act	22 October 1970
Cayman Islands Stock Exchange	4 March 2004
China	
Hong Kong – Any stock exchange recognised under Section 2A(1) of the Hong Kong Companies Ordinance	26 February 1971
Denmark	
Copenhagen Stock Exchange	22 October 1970
Finland	
Helsinki Stock Exchange	22 October 1970
France[3]	22 October 1970
Germany[3]	5 August 1971
Greece	
Athens Stock Exchange	14 June 1993
Guernsey[3]	10 December 2002
Iceland	31 March 2006
Irish Republic[3]	22 October 1970
Italy[3]	3 May 1972
Japan[3]	22 October 1970
Korea	10 October 1994
Luxembourg[3]	21 February 1972
Malaysia	
Kuala Lumpur Stock Exchange	10 October 1994
Malta Stock Exchange	29 December 2005
Mexico	10 October 1994
Netherlands[3]	22 October 1970
New Zealand	22 September 1988
Norway[3]	22 October 1970
Portugal[3]	21 February 1972
Singapore	30 June 1977
South Africa	
Bond Exchange of South Africa	16 April 2008
Johannesburg Stock Exchange	22 October 1970
Spain[3]	5 August 1971
Sri Lanka	
Colombo Stock Exchange	21 February 1972
Sweden	
Stockholm Stock Exchange	16 July 1985
Swiss Stock Exchange	12 May 1997
Thailand	10 October 1994
United Kingdom	19 July 2007
United States	
Any stock exchange registered with the SEC as a national securities exchange[1]	22 October 1970
Nasdaq Stock Market[2]	10 March 1992

[1] 'National securities exchange' does not include any local exchanges registered with Securities and Exchange Commission.

[2] As maintained through the facilities of the National Association of Securities Dealers Inc and its subsidiaries.

[3] Ie, a stock exchange according to the law of the country concerned relating to stock exchanges.

Recognised futures exchanges

The following is a list of exchanges which have been designated as recognised futures exchanges under TCGA 1992 s 288(6). By concession, those exchanges were recognised futures exchanges for the tax year of recognition onwards.

Recognised futures exchanges	Date of recognition
International Petroleum Exchange of London	6.8.85
London Metal Exchange	6.8.85
London Gold Market	12.12.85
London Silver Market	12.12.85
CME Group (formerly Chicago Mercantile Exchange and Chicago Board of Trade)	19.12.86
New York Mercantile Exchange	19.12.86
Philadelphia Board of Trade	19.12.86
Mid America Commodity Exchange	29.7.87
Montreal Exchange	29.7.87
Hong Kong Futures Exchange	15.12.87
Commodity Exchange (Comex)	25.8.88
Sydney Futures Exchange	13.10.88
Euronext (London International Financial Futures and Options Exchange)	22.3.92
OM Stockholm	18.3.92
OM London	18.3.92
New York Board of Trade	10.6.04

Recognised investment exchanges and clearing houses

The following is a list of investment exchanges and clearing houses recognised as investment exchanges under the Financial Services and Markets Act 2000 and able to carry out investment business in the UK.

Recognised investment exchanges	Date of recognition
London Stock Exchange	22 November 2001
International Petroleum Exchange of London	5 April 1988
LIFFE Administration and Management	22 November 2001
London Metal Exchange	22 November 2001
Virt-x Exchange Ltd	23 November 2001
ICE Futures	22 November 2001
EDX London Ltd	1 July 2003
NYMEX Europe	7 September 2005

Recognised clearing houses	Date of recognition
CH Clearnet	23 November 2001
CRESTCo	23 November 2001

Recognised overseas investment exchanges and clearing houses

The following is a list of overseas investment exchanges and clearing houses recognised under the Financial Services and Markets Act 2000 and able to conduct investment business in the UK.

Recognised overseas investment exchange	Date of recognition
National Association of Securities Dealers Automated Quotations (NASDAQ)	23 November 2001
Sydney Futures Exchange	30 January 2002
Chicago Mercantile Exchange (CME)	23 November 2001
Chicago Board of Trade (CBOT)	23 November 2001
New York Mercantile Exchange (NYMEX)	23 November 2001
NQLX LLC	23 November 2001
Swiss Stock Exchange (SWX)	23 November 2001
Cantor Financial Futures Exchange (CFEE)	23 November 2001
EUREX Zurich	23 November 2001
Warenterminborse Hannover	23 November 2001
US Futures Exchange	21 May 2004

Recognised clearing house	Date of recognition
SIS x-clear AG	19 August 2004

Applications for clearances and approvals

Clearance application	Address
Transfer of long-term insurance business (TCGA 1992 s 211, TA 1988 s 444A)	Richard Thomas, CT & VAT Product & Process (Insurance Group), 3rd (3C/10) Floor, 100 Parliament Street, London SW1A 2BQ
Demergers (TA 1988 s 215); Company purchase of own shares (TA 1988 s 225); Transactions in securities (TA 1988 s 707; ITA 2007 s 701); Enterprise Investment Scheme – acquisition of shares by new company (ITA 2007 s 247(1)(f)); Share exchanges (TCGA 1992 ss 138, 139, 140B, 140D); and Intangible fixed assets (FA 2002 Sch 29 para 88)	Clearance and Counteraction Team, Anti-Avoidance Team, First Floor, 22 Kingsway, London WC2B 6NR (Market sensitive applications to Eric Gardner; non-market sensitive applications to Mohini Sawhney – see note below)[1]
Company migration (FA 1988 s 130)	Hazel Ford, CT & VAT (International CT), 100 Parliament Street, London SW1A 2BQ
Advance pricing agreements (FA 1999 ss 85–87)	Ian Wood, CT & VAT (International CT), 100 Parliament Street, London SW1A 2BQ
	For APAs involving oil taxation: Alan Tume or Malcolm Phelps, Large Business Service Oil & Gas (APAs), 2nd Floor, 22 Kingsway, London WC2B 6 NRL
Controlled foreign companies (TA 1988 ss 747–756, Schs 24–26)	Mary Sharp/David Price/Des Hanna, CT & VAT (International CT), 100 Parliament Street, London SW1A 2BQ
Corporate Venturing Schemes (FA 2000 Sch 15)	Small Company Enterprise Centre, CRI, Ty Glas, Llanishen, Cardiff CF14 5ZG

[1] Where clearance is sought under any one or more of TA 1988 ss 215, 225, 304A, 707; TCGA 1992 ss 138, 139, 140B, 140D; or FA 2002 Sch 29 para 88, clearance applications may be sent in a single letter to the above London address for clearances under those sections. The letter should make clear what clearance is required. E-mail applications can be sent to reconstructions@hmrc.gsi.gov.uk and fax applications to 020 7438 4409. For market sensitive information, call Eric Gardner on 020 7438 6585 before sending an e-mail or fax. A reply by e-mail should be requested if required. General enquiries can be made to Mohini Sawhney on 020 7438 8355.

[2] Non-statutory clearances: Businesses may apply for a non-statutory clearance where there is material uncertainty and the issue is commercially significant. Such requests for clearance should be sent to the Client Relationship Manager or the HMRC Clearances Team, Alexander House, 21 Victoria Avenue, Southend-on-Sea, Essex SS99 1BD.

Approval application	Address
Pensions (TA 1988 ss 590, 591)	HMRC, Pension Schemes Office, Yorke House, PO Box 62, Castle Meadow Road, Nottingham NG2 1BG
Employee share schemes (ITEPA 2003 Schs 2,3,4)	HMRC Employee Shares & Securities Unit, Room G52, 100 Parliament Street, London SW1A 2BQ
Qualifying life assurance policies (TA 1988 Sch 15)	Claire Ritchie, Revenue Policy, Business Tax (Insurance), Third Floor (3C/09), 100 Parliament Street, London SW1A 2BQ
Professional bodies (relief for subscriptions) (ITEPA 2003 s 343)	A list of approved professional bodies and learned societies is available on the HMRC website (at www.hmrc.gov.uk/list3/index.htm)

Application for treasury consent	Address
Transactions in shares or debentures (TA 1988 ss 765, 765A)	Des Hanna/David Price/Ian Wright (s 765) Mark Bryan (s 765A), CT & VAT (International CT), 100 Parliament Street, London SW1A 2BQ

Confirmation or pre-transaction advice	Address
Funding issues (TA 1988 ss 209, 703)	Miles Nelson, CT & VAT (International CT), 100 Parliament Street, London SW1A 2BQ
Transactions in land (TA 1988 ss 35, 776)	Applications for clearance should be sent to the HMRC Officer who deals with the returns

Capital allowances

Rates

Agricultural buildings

	Expenditure incurred after	% Rate
Initial allowance	31 October 1992[1]	20
	31 October 1993	Nil
Writing-down allowance	**31 March 1986 and before 6 April 2011(1 April 2011 for companies)**	4[2],[3]

[1] Initial allowances were temporarily reintroduced for 1 year in respect of capital expenditure on agricultural buildings or works. The allowances applied to buildings or works constructed under a contract entered into between 1 November 1992 and 31 October 1993, and brought into use for the purposes of the farming trade by 31 December 1994. See CAA 1990 s 124A.

[2] Agricultural buildings allowances are to be abolished for income tax purposes for 2011/12 onwards and for corporation tax purposes for the financial year beginning 1 April 2011 onwards. (FA 2008, s 84)

[3] As a transitional measure, writing-down allowances are being stepped down over the three financial or tax years prior to abolition. For 2008/09 (for corporation tax, the financial year beginning 1 April 2008) only 75% of the allowance is given. For 2009/10 (or financial year beginning 1 April 2009) only 50% is given and for 2010/11 (or financial year beginning 1 April 2010) only 25%. Where a chargeable period falls in more than one tax or financial year, time apportionment applies to determine the amount of the allowance. (FA 2008, s 85)

Note: For balancing events on or after 21 March 2007, no election for a balancing adjustment can be made so that the new holder of the relevant interest will, in all cases, calculate writing-down allowances based on the previous owner's balance of qualifying expenditure (cost less allowances claimed).

Dredging

	Expenditure incurred after	% Rate
Writing-down allowance	**5 November 1962**	4

Industrial buildings and structures

	Expenditure[1] incurred after	% Rate
Initial allowance		
Generally:	31 October 1992	20
	31 October 1993	Nil
Exception: Enterprise zones	**within 10 years of site being included in zone[2]**	100
Writing-down allowance		
Generally:	**5 April 1946**	2
	5 November 1962[3]and before 6 April 2011 (1 April 2011 for companies)[6],[7]	4
Exception: Enterprise zones	**within 10 years of site being included in zone[4]**	25

[1] The amount qualifying for allowance is the price paid for the relevant interest *minus* (i) the value of the land element and (ii) any value attributable to elements over and above those which would feature in a normal commercial lease negotiated in the open market: FA 1995 s 100 confirming previous practice.

[2] CAA 2001 s 306. Includes expenditure on qualifying hotels. See p 24 for enterprise zones.

[3] Includes expenditure on qualifying hotels (other than in an enterprise zone).

Also includes expenditure on the construction of toll roads incurred for accounting periods or basis periods ending after 5 April 1991.

[4] CAA 2001 s 310. Includes expenditure on qualifying hotels. See p 24 for enterprise zones.

[5] For balancing events on or after 21 March 2007, no balancing adjustment will arise and the new holder of the relevant interest will calculate writing-down allowances based on the previous owner's balance of qualifying expenditure (cost less allowances claimed).

[6] Industrial buildings allowances and allowances for buildings in enterprise zones are to be abolished for income tax purposes for 2011/12 onwards and for corporation tax purposes for the financial year beginning 1 April 2011 onwards. (FA 2008, s 84, 86)

[7] As a transitional measure, writing-down allowances are being stepped down over the three financial or tax years prior to abolition. For 2008/09 (for corporation tax, the financial year beginning 1 April 2008) only 75% of the allowance is given. For 2009/10 (or financial year beginning 1 April 2009) only 50% is given and for 2010/11 (or financial year beginning 1 April 2010) only 25%. Where a chargeable period falls in more than one tax or financial year, time apportionment applies to determine the amount of the allowance. (FA 2008, s 85, 87)

Flat conversions

Initial allowance	Expenditure incurred after	% Rate
	10 May 2001	100

Applies to expenditure incurred on renovating or converting vacant or storage space above commercial properties to provide low value flats for rent. A writing-down allowance is given at 25% (on a straight-line basis) on unrelieved expenditure. (CAA 2001 ss 393A–393W; FA 2001 s 67, Sch 19).

Know-how

Expenditure incurred after 31 March 1986: annual 25% writing-down allowance (reducing balance basis).

Plant and machinery

Expenditure incurred	after	before	Up to pa
Annual investment allowance[1]			
for income tax purposes	5 April 2008		£50,000
for corporation tax purposes	31 March 2008		£50,000
First-year allowance (FYA)			
Small and medium-sized businesses[2]			% Rate
for income tax purposes	1 July 1998	6 April 2008	40
for corporation tax purposes	1 July 1998	1 April 2008	40
	1 July 1997	2 July 1998	50/12
in Northern Ireland *only*	11 May 1998	12 May 2002	100
Small businesses[3]			
for income tax purposes	5 April 2006	6 April 2008	50
	5 April 2004	6 April 2005	50
for corporation tax purposes	31 March 2006	1 April 2008	50
	31 March 2004	1 April 2005	50
ICT	31 March 2000	1 April 2004	100
Energy-saving plant or machinery[4]	31 March 2001		100
New low-emission cars and refuelling equipment[5]	16 April 2002	1 April 2013	100
Environmentally beneficial plant or machinery[6]	31 March 2003		100
Long life assets			
for income tax purposes	5 April 2008		10
for corporation tax purposes	31 March 2008		10
for income tax purposes		6 April 2008	6
for corporation tax purposes		1 April 2008	6
Integral features[9]			
for income tax purposes	5 April 2008		10
for corporation tax purposes	31 March 2008		10
Thermal insulation			
for income tax purposes	5 April 2008		10
for corporation tax purposes	31 March 2008		10
Foreign leased assets[10]	9 March 1982	1 April 2006	10
Writing-down allowance (WDA)[7]			
Generally	26 October 1970	1 or 6 April 2008	25
	Accounting periods starting on or after		
for income tax purposes	6 April 2008		20
for corporation tax	1 April 2008		20
	Accounting periods straddling		
for income tax	6 April 2008		Hybrid rate[7]
for corporation tax	1 April 2008		Hybrid rate[7]

1.   The first £50,000 of qualifying expenditure incurred in a chargeable period qualifies for the annual investment allowance at 100%. The limit is proportionately increased or decreased where the chargeable period is longer or shorter than a year. A group of companies (defined as for company law purposes) can only receive a single allowance. This restriction also applies to certain related businesses or companies. Expenditure on cars does not qualify. (FA 2008, s 74, Sch 24).

2.   **Small and medium-sized businesses:** The allowance does not apply to certain expenditure including that on plant and machinery for leasing, motor cars, ships, railway assets or long-life assets. After the first year, allowances revert to the normal WDA. The rate of 50% applied only for expenditure incurred during the year ended 1 July 1998 when a 12% FYA applied to long-life assets. (See notes 4 and 11 below.) Small and medium-sized businesses are, broadly, those satisfying any two of the following conditions: (a) turnover £22,800,000 or less (b) assets £11,400,000 or less (c) not more than 250 employees (CAA 1990 ss 22(3C), (6B), 22A, 44, 46–49). For accounting periods ending before 30.01.04, the thresholds were: (a) turnover £11,200,000 or less (b) assets £5,600,000 or less.

3.   **Small businesses:** See note 2 above for conditions for relief. Small businesses are, broadly, those satisfying any two of the following conditions: (a) turnover £5,600,000 or less (b) assets £2,800,000 or less (c) not more than 50 employees. For accounting periods ending before 30.01.04, the thresholds were: (a) turnover £2,800,000 or less (b) assets £1,400,000 or less. (FA 2004 s 142).

4.   **Energy-saving plant or machinery:** The allowances are available for investment by *any* business in designated energy-saving plant and machinery in accordance with the Government's Energy Technology Product List (CAA 2001 ss 45A–45C, 46; FA 2001 s 65, Sch 17; SI 2001/2541; SI 2005/1114). The product lists are available at www.eca.gov.uk.

5.   **Low-emission cars:** The allowance is given on (a) new cars which are either electrically propelled or emit not more than 110g/km of carbon dioxide (120g/km for expenditure incurred before 1 April 2008), registered after 16 April 2002 and (b) new plant and machinery to refuel vehicles in a gas refuelling station with natural gas, hydrogen fuels, or (for expenditure on or after 1 April 2008) biogas (CAA 2001 ss 45D, 45E, 46).

6.   **Environmentally beneficial plant or machinery:** Allowances are available for expenditure by *any* business on new and unused designated technologies and products which satisfy the relevant environmental criteria in accordance with the Government's technologies or products lists (FA 2003 s 167, Sch 30). The product lists are available at www.eca.gov.uk.

7.   **WDAs** are calculated on a reducing balance basis. For chargeable periods beginning before 6 April 2008 and ending on or after that date (or, for corporation tax purposes, beginning before 1 April 2008 and ending on or after that date) a hybrid rate of WDAs applies, calculated by time apportionment of the 25% and 20% rates, for the long-life asset pool, the 6% and 10% rates. For chargeable periods beginning on or after 6 April 2008 (1 April 2008 for corporation tax purposes), a WDA of up to £1,000 can be claimed in respect of the main pool and/or the special rate pool where the unrelieved expenditure in the pool concerned is £1,000 or less.

8.   **Long-life assets:** Applies to plant or machinery with an expected working life, when new, of 25 years or more. Applies where expenditure on long-life assets in a year is £100,000 or more (in the case of companies the de minimis limit is £100,000 divided by one plus the number of associated companies). Transitional provisions apply to maintain a 25% allowance for expenditure incurred before 1 January 2001 under a contract entered into before 26 November 1996 and to expenditure on second-hand plant or machinery if old rules applied to vendor. It does not apply to plant or machinery in a building used wholly or mainly as, or for purposes ancillary to, a dwelling-house, retail shop, showroom, hotel or office, cars, or sea-going ships and railway assets acquired before 1 January 2011. Expenditure on or after 1 or 6 April 2008 qualifies, as special rate expenditure, for a writing down allowance of 10% reducing balance. The balance of the long-life asset pool at 1 or 6 April is also transferred into the special rate pool. (CAA 2001 ss 90–104, Sch 3 para 20).

9.   Integral features of a building are electrical systems (including lighting systems); cold water systems; space or water heating systems, powered ventilation systems, air cooling or purification and any floor or ceiling comprised in such systems; lifts, escalators and moving walkways and external solar shading. They all fall into the special rate pool and qualify for a 10% writing down allowance. (CAA 2001, ss 104E) Whenever possible, a claim or election must be made on the tax return or by an amendment to the return (TMA 1970 s 42 and FA 1998 Sch 18 paras 9, 10, 67 and 79). Exceptions to this general rule are dealt with in TMA 1970 Sch 1A. Except where another period is expressly prescribed, a claim for relief in respect of income tax and capital gains tax must be made within five years from the 31 January following the year of assessment to which it relates. From a date to be appointed, the time limit is to be changed to four years after the end of the tax year. (TMA 1970 s 43(1) as amended and FA 2008 Sch 39 para 12).

10.   The relief applies only to leases finalised before 1 April 2006 (CAA 2001 s 109; FA 2006 Sch 9 para 13).

11.   First-year tax credits: For expenditure incurred on or after 1 April 2008, a company can surrender a tax loss attributable to first-year allowances for energy saving or environmentally friendly equipment in exchange for a cash payment from the Government. The cash payment is equal to 19% of the loss surrendered, subject to an upper limit of the greater of £250,000 and the company's PAYE and NIC liability for the period concerned. (CAA 2001 Sch A1)

Cars: Car and motorcycle hire p 51.

Mineral extraction

First-year allowance: 100% FYA is available for certain expenditure incurred after 16 April 2002 wholly for the purposes of a North Sea Oil ring-fence trade or on plant and machinery used in such a trade.
Writing-down allowance: for expenditure incurred after 31 March 1986, 10% for expenditure on the acquisition of a mineral asset and certain pre-trading expenditure, otherwise 25% (on reducing balance basis). (CA 2001 s 418)

Motor cars

Available for private use

	Expenditure incurred after	% Rate
Writing-down allowance (WDA)	11 March 1992	**25%**
	1 April 2008 corporation tax or 5 April 2008 income tax	**20%**[1]

[1] Restricted to £3,000 for cars costing more than £12,000 and bought outright, on hire purchase or by way of a lease with an option to purchase (CAA 2001 ss 74, 75).
[2] The requirement that expenditure on cars costing £12,000 or less goes into a separate pool was removed from the start of the chargeable period which includes 1 April 2000 (corporation tax) or 6 April 2000 (income tax) or the start of the chargeable period which includes 1 (or 6) April 2001 at the option of the taxpayer (CAA 1990 s 41; FA 2000 s 74).
[3] See also note 5, p 23 and Car hire, p 51.

Patent rights

Writing-down allowance
Expenditure incurred after 31 March 1986: annual 25% writing-down allowance (reducing balance basis). (CA 2001 s 472)

Research and development (formerly scientific research)

	Expenditure incurred after	% Rate
Allowance in year 1	5 November 1962	**100**

Note: Land and houses are excluded from 1 April 1985. See also corporation tax relief, p 45.

Disadvantaged areas

Renovation of business premises

	Expenditure incurred on or after	% Rate
First-year allowance	11 April 2007	**100**

The expenditure must be incurred on renovating or converting vacant business properties in Northern Ireland or the designated disadvantaged areas in the UK that have been vacant for at least a year, to bring the property back into business use. (Premises refurbished by or used by businesses in the following trades are excluded from the scheme: fisheries and aquaculture, shipbuilding, the coal or steel industries, synthetic fibres, primary production of certain agricultural products and the manufacture of products which imitate or substitute for milk or milk products.) The enhanced rate will apply to any expenditure currently qualifying for plant and machinery, industrial buildings or agricultural buildings allowances and also to expenditure on commercial buildings (such as shops and offices). A writing-down allowance is given at 25% (on a straight-line basis) on unrelieved expenditure. (FA 2005 s 92, Sch 6).

Enterprise zones

Before 1 April 2011 (6 April 2011 for individuals) an initial allowance of 100% is available for expenditure on industrial or commercial building by businesses within enterprise zones. Where the initial allowance is not or is only partially claimed a 25% writing-down allowance on cost, on a straight-line basis, applies to the unclaimed balance. There is no phasing out of the allowance between 2008 and 2011.

Capital gains

Annual exemption

Individuals,[a] personal representatives[b] and certain trusts[c]

Exempt amount of net gains	2003–04	2004–05	2005–06	2006–07	2007–08	2008–09
	£7,900	£8,200	£8,500	£8,800	£9,200	**£9,600**

[a] For 2008–09 onwards, an individual who claims to use the remittance basis for a tax year is not entitled to the capital gains tax annual exemption for that year. This does not apply if the individual's unremitted foreign income and gains for the year are less than £2,000.

[b] Year of death and following two years (maximum).

[c] Trusts for mentally disabled persons and those in receipt of attendance allowance or disability living allowance. Exemption divided by number of qualifying settlements created (after 9 March 1981) by one settlor, subject to a minimum of one-tenth.

Trusts[a] generally

Exempt amount of net gains	2003–04	2004–05	2005–05	2006–07	2007–08	2008–09
	£3,950	£4,100	£4,250	£4,400	£4,600	**£4,800**

[a] Exemption divided by number of qualifying settlements created (after 6 June 1978) by one settlor, subject to a minimum of one-fifth.

Chattel exemption

	Disposals exemption	Marginal relief: Maximum chargeable gain
From 1989–90 onwards	£6,000	5/3 excess over £6,000

Rates of tax

2008–09	*Individuals, trusts and personal representatives*			18%
2007–08	*Individuals*	•	to income tax starting rate limit £2,230	10%
		•	from £2,231 to income tax basic rate limit £34,600	20%
		•	above income tax basic rate limit £34,600	40%
	Trusts and personal representatives			40%
2006–07	*Individuals*	•	to income tax starting rate limit £2,150	10%
		•	from £2,151 to income tax basic rate limit £33,300	20%
		•	above income tax basic rate limit £33,300	40%
	Trusts and personal representatives			40%
2004–05 to 2005–06	*Individuals*	•	to income tax starting rate limit	10%
		•	above starting rate limit to income tax basic rate limit	20%
		•	above income tax basic rate limit	40%
	Trusts and personal representatives			40%
2000–01 to 2003–04	*Individuals*	•	to income tax starting rate limit	10%
		•	above starting rate limit to income tax basic rate limit	20%
		•	above income tax basic rate limit	40%
	Trusts and personal representatives			34%
Gains are taxed on individuals as the top slice of income.				
Trusts for vulnerable persons: From 2004–05 onwards, gains taxed at beneficiary's rates (on beneficiary if UK resident or on trustees if beneficiary not UK-resident).				
Settlements where settlor retains an interest: chargeable on settlor at own rates. Adjustment is necessary for savings income (including interest from banks and building societies, interest distributions from authorised unit trusts, interest from gilts and other securities including corporate bonds, purchased life annuities, and discounts). Adjustment is also necessary for dividends or other qualifying distributions from a UK-resident company.				

Indexation allowance – individuals

(TCGA 1992 ss 53–57, 109)

Indexation allowance is abolished for disposals on or after 6 April 2008 by individuals, trustees and personal representatives (but not companies). For disposals before that date by such persons, an indexation allowance is given up to April 1998 and taper relief applies thereafter on disposals made after 5 April 1998 (see below). Indexation allowance is deducted before applying taper relief. The indexation allowance is calculated by multiplying each item of allowable expenditure by:

$$\frac{RD - RI}{RI}$$

where:

RD is the retail prices index figure for month of disposal;

RI is the retail prices index for month of expenditure (or March 1982 if later).

See pp 31–43 for indexation allowances applicable for corporation tax and p 44 for RPI values.

For disposals after 31 March 1998 of assets acquired on or before that date the factors below can be used to calculate the indexation allowance available to April 1998 for acquisitions in the month shown.

	Jan	Feb	Mar	Apr	May	Jun	Jul	Aug	Sep	Oct	Nov	Dec
1982	–	–	1·047	1·006	0·992	0·987	0·986	0·985	0·987	0·977	0·967	0·971
1983	0·968	0·960	0·956	0·929	0·921	0·917	0·906	0·898	0·889	0·883	0·876	0·871
1984	0·872	0·865	0·859	0·834	0·828	0·823	0·825	0·808	0·804	0·793	0·788	0·789
1985	0·783	0·769	0·752	0·716	0·708	0·704	0·707	0·703	0·704	0·701	0·695	0·693
1986	0·689	0·683	0·681	0·665	0·662	0·663	0·667	0·662	0·654	0·652	0·638	0·632
1987	0·626	0·620	0·616	0·597	0·596	0·596	0·597	0·593	0·588	0·580	0·573	0·574
1988	0·574	0·568	0·562	0·537	0·531	0·525	0·524	0·507	0·500	0·485	0·478	0·474
1989	0·465	0·454	0·448	0·423	0·414	0·409	0·408	0·404	0·395	0·384	0·372	0·369
1990	0·361	0·353	0·339	0·300	0·288	0·283	0·282	0·269	0·258	0·248	0·251	0·252
1991	0·249	0·242	0·237	0·222	0·218	0·213	0·215	0·213	0·208	0·204	0·199	0·198
1992	0·199	0·193	0·189	0·171	0·167	0·167	0·171	0·171	0·166	0·162	0·164	0·168
1993	0·179	0·171	0·167	0·156	0·152	0·153	0·156	0·151	0·146	0·147	0·148	0·146
1994	0·151	0·144	0·141	0·128	0·124	0·124	0·129	0·124	0·121	0·120	0·119	0·114
1995	0·114	0·107	0·102	0·091	0·087	0·085	0·091	0·085	0·080	0·085	0·085	0·079
1996	0·083	0·078	0·073	0·066	0·063	0·063	0·067	0·062	0·057	0·057	0·057	0·053
1997	0·053	0·049	0·046	0·040	0·036	0·032	0·032	0·026	0·021	0·019	0·019	0·016
1998	0·019	0·014	0·011	–	–	–	–	–	–	–	–	–

Losses. For disposals after 30 November 1993, indexation allowance can only be used to reduce or extinguish a gain. It cannot be used to create or increase a capital loss.

Share identification rules

(TCGA 1992 ss 104–106A; FA 2006 s 74)

For disposals on or after 6 April 2008 by individuals, trustees or personal representatives, shares and securities of the same class in the same company are identified with acquisitions in the following order:

- acquisitions on the same day as the disposal;
- acquisitions within 30 days after the day of disposal;
- shares comprised in a single pool incorporating all other shares of the same class, whenever acquired.

For acquisitions after 5 April 1998 and before 5 April 2008 for individuals, trustees and personal representatives, disposals are identified with acquisitions in the following order:

- same day acquisitions (subject to special rules distinguishing shares acquired after 5 April 2002 from approved employee share option schemes from other shares acquired on the same day);
- acquisitions within the following 30 days[1] (thus countering 'bed and breakfasting');
- previous acquisitions after 5 April 1998 on a last in/first out basis;
- shares acquired after 5 April 1982 in the pool at 5 April 1998 (the 'section 104 holding');
- shares acquired before 6 April 1982 (the '1982 holding');
- any shares acquired on or before 6 April 1965 on a last in/first out basis;
- if any shares disposed of are still not fully matched, shares acquired subsequent to the disposal (beyond the above mentioned 30-day period).

For the purposes of corporation tax on chargeable gains, disposals of shares etc are identified with acquisitions in the following order:

- same day acquisitions;
- acquisitions within the previous nine days on a first in/first out basis;
- the pool of shares acquired after 31 March 1982;
- any shares held at 31 March 1982;
- any shares acquired on or before 6 April 1965 on a last in/first out basis;
- (if shares disposed of still not fully matched) subsequent acquisitions.

These rules are modified for disposals of shares before 5 December 2005 if the company acquired shares of the same class within a short period and held not less than 2% of the number issued.

[1] The 30-day matching rule does not apply in relation to acquisitions after 21 March 2006 where the individual making the disposal is not (or is not treated as) resident or ordinarily resident in the UK at the time of the acquisition.

Entrepreneur's relief

(FA 2008, s 9, Sch 3)

Entrepreneur's relief applies to disposals by an individual on or after 6 April 2008 of:
- all or part of a trade carried on alone or in partnership;
- assets of such a trade following cessation; or
- shares or securities in the individual's 'personal trading company (as defined).

Where a disposal of shares or of an interest in the assets of a partnership qualifies for relief, an associated disposal of assets owned by the individual and used by the company or partnership also qualifies for relief. Trustees can claim relief where a qualifying beneficiary has an interest in the business concerned.

The relief is available where the relevant conditions are met throughout a period of one year and operates by reducing the amount of qualifying gains by four-ninths (so that the gains are effectively charged to CGT at 10%). Relief is subject to a lifetime limit of gains of £1 million, but disposals before 6 April 2008 do not count towards the limit. Relief given to trustees counts towards the limit of the qualifying beneficiary.

Transitional rules apply to allow relief to be claimed in certain circumstances where a gain made before 6 April 2008 is deferred and becomes chargeable on or after that date.

Taper relief

(TCGA 1992 s 2A, Sch A1; FA 2000 ss 66, 67; FA 2002 ss 46, 47, Sch 10; FA 2003 s 160)

Taper relief is abolished for gains accruing, or treated as accruing, on or after 6 April 2008. (FA 2008 Sch 2 para 25). Taper relief was available for disposals made after 5 April 1998 by individuals, trustees and personal representatives. The chargeable gain is reduced according to the number of complete years for which the asset has been held (counting from 6 April 1998). Non-business assets acquired before 17 March 1998 qualify for an addition of one year to the period for which they are held after 5 April 1998. Business assets acquired before 17 March 1998 also qualify for the one-year addition but only if disposed of before 6 April 2000.

Taper relief applies to gains after all deductions and before the annual exemption. Losses are set against pre-tapered gains in the most beneficial way possible. Where applicable, the combined period of holding by spouses is taken into account.

Business assets			
Disposals from 6 April 2002		*Disposals from 6 April 2000 to 5 April 2002*	
No of complete yrs from 6.4.98 for which asset held	*% of gain chargeable*	*No of complete yrs from 6.4.98 for which asset held*	*% of gain chargeable*
		0	100
0	100	1	87.5
1	50	2	75
2 or more	25	3	50
		4 or more	25

Non-business assets			
No of complete yrs from 6.4.98 for which asset held	*% of gain chargeable*	*No of complete yrs from 6.4.98 for which asset held*	*% of gain chargeable*
0	100	6	80
1	100	7	75
2	100	8	70
3	95	9	65
4	90	10 or more	60
5	85		

Business assets. A 'business asset' is one of the following:
- an asset used for the purposes of a trade carried on (alone or in partnership) by the taxpayer or, after 5 April 2004, any individual, trustee or personal representative; or
- an asset used for the purposes of a trade carried on by a 'qualifying company' (alone or, after 4 April 2004, in partnership); or
- shares or securities in a 'qualifying company'; or
- from 6 April 2000, an asset used for the purpose of any office or employment (full-time or part-time) held by the taxpayer with a person carrying on a trade; or
- before 6 April 2000, an asset held for the purposes of a qualifying office or employment to which the taxpayer is required to devote substantially the whole of his time.

Qualifying company. From 6 April 2000, a *'qualifying company'*, by reference to an individual, is a trading company (or holding company of a trading group), where one or more of the following conditions is met:
- the company is unlisted (including an AIM company); or
- the taxpayer is an employee (full-time or part-time) of the company or a fellow group company (in which case the requirement that the company be a trading company etc is dropped, provided the taxpayer's interest in the company, including connected person holdings, is no more than 10%); or
- the taxpayer can exercise at least 5% of the voting rights.

Leases

Depreciation table (TCGA 1992 Sch 8 para 1)

Yrs	%	Yrs	%	Yrs	%
50 (or more)	100	33	90·280	16	64·116
49	99·657	32	89·354	15	61·617
48	99·289	31	88·371	14	58·971
47	98·902	30	87·330	13	56·167
46	98·490	29	86·226	12	53·191
45	98·059	28	85·053	11	50·038
44	97·595	27	83·816	10	46·695
43	97·107	26	82·496	9	43·154
42	96·593	25	81·100	8	39·399
41	96·041	24	79·622	7	35·414
40	95·457	23	78·055	6	31·195
39	94·842	22	76·399	5	26·722
38	94·189	21	74·635	4	21·983
37	93·497	20	72·770	3	16·959
36	92·761	19	70·791	2	11·629
35	91·981	18	68·697	1	5·983
34	91·156	17	66·470	0	0

Formula: Fraction of expenditure disallowed—

$$\frac{AE - D}{AE}$$

Where:

AE is the percentage for duration of lease at acquisition or expenditure; and

D is the percentage for duration of lease at disposal.

Fractions of years: Add one-twelfth of the difference between the percentage for the whole year and the next higher percentage for each additional month. Odd days under 14 are not counted; 14 odd days or more count as a month.

Short leases: premiums treated as rent (TA 1988 s 34, TCGA 1992 Sch 8 para 5; ITTOIA 2005 ss 277–281) Part of premium for grant of a short lease which is chargeable to income tax as property income:

$$P - (2\% \times (n - 1) \times P)$$

Where:

P is the amount of premium;

n is the number of complete years which lease has to run when granted.

Length of lease (complete years)	Amount chargeable to CGT %	Income tax charge %	Length of lease (complete years)	Amount chargeable to CGT %	Income tax charge %	Length of lease (complete years)	Amount chargeable to CGT %	Income tax charge %
Over 50	100	0	34	66	34	17	32	68
50	98	2	33	64	36	16	30	70
49	96	4	32	62	38	15	28	72
48	94	6	31	60	40	14	26	74
47	92	8	30	58	42	13	24	76
46	90	10	29	56	44	12	22	78
45	88	12	28	54	46	11	20	80
44	86	14	27	52	48	10	18	82
43	84	16	26	50	50	9	16	84
42	82	18	25	48	52	8	14	86
41	80	20	24	46	54	7	12	88
40	78	22	23	44	56	6	10	90
39	76	24	22	42	58	5	8	92
38	74	26	21	40	60	4	6	94
37	72	28	20	38	62	3	4	96
36	70	30	19	36	64	2	2	98
35	68	32	18	34	66	1 or less	0	100

Reliefs

The following is a summary of the other main capital gains tax reliefs and exemptions.

Charities

Gains accruing to charities which are both applicable and applied for charitable purposes are exempt. The exemption was extended from 6 April 2002 to donations to Community Amateur Sports Clubs (CASCs)

Individuals

Compensation (injury to person, profession or vocation)	Exempt
Decorations for valour (acquired otherwise than for money or money's worth)	Gain exempt
Enterprise Investment Scheme (see p 62)	Gain on disposal after relevant three-year period exempt to extent full relief given on shares
Entrepreneurs relief (see p 27)	Five ninths of gains on specified assets chargeable at 18% (an effective rate of 10%) up to lifetime limit of £1 million
Foreign currency acquired for personal expenditure	Gain exempt
Gifts for public benefit, works of art, historic buildings etc	No chargeable gain/allowable loss
Gilt-edged stock	No chargeable gain/allowable loss
Hold-over relief for gifts	Restricted to: (1) gifts of business assets (including unquoted shares in trading companies and holding companies of trading groups). Relief is not available on the transfer of shares or securities to a company made after 8 November 1999 (other than transfers between 6.4.03 and 20.10.03) (2) gifts of heritage property (3) gifts to heritage maintenance funds (4) gifts to political parties, and (5) gifts which are chargeable transfers for inheritance tax. Where available, transferee's acquisition cost treated as reduced by held-over gain.
Married persons or civil partners living together	No chargeable gain/allowable loss on transfers between spouses or civil partners
Motor vehicles	Gain exempt
Principal private residence	Gain exempt
If residence is partly let, exemption for the let part is limited to the smaller of—	(1) exemption on owner-occupied part (2) and £40,000
Qualifying corporate bonds	No chargeable gain (for loans made before 17 March 1998, allowable loss in certain cases if all or part of loss is irrecoverable)
Retirement relief (phased out from 6 April 1999 and no longer available for disposals after 5 April 2003)	Available for disposals (minimum age of retirement 50) after: 5 April 2002 — 100% relief on gains up to £50,000 / 50% relief on gains of £50,000.01–£200,000 / maximum relief of £125,000 5 April 2001 — 100% relief on gains up to £100,000 / 50% relief on gains of £100,000.01–£400,000 / maximum relief of £250,000 5 April 2000 — 100% relief on gains up to £150,000 / 50% relief on gains of £150,000.01–£600,000 / maximum relief of £375,000
Venture capital trusts (see p 62)	Gain on disposal of shares by original investor exempt if company still a venture capital trust. Exemption applies only to shares acquired up to the permitted maximum of £200,000 per year of assessment (£100,000 for shares acquired before 6 April 2004). Deferral relief is available on gains on assets where the disposal proceeds are reinvested in VCT shares issued before 6 April 2004 and within one year before or after the disposal. This relief is withdrawn for shares issued after that date.

Businesses

Roll-over relief for replacement of business assets
Qualifying assets:
- Buildings and land both occupied and used for the purposes of the trade.
- Fixed plant and machinery.
- Ships, aircraft and hovercraft.
- Satellites, space stations and spacecraft.
- Goodwill.
  * From 1 April 2002 onwards, subject to transitional rules, these items are removed from the list for companies only (as they fall within the intangible assets regime from that date (FA 2002 Sch 29 para 132(5))).
- Milk and potato quotas*.
- Ewe and suckler cow premium quotas*.
- Fish quotas (from 29 March 1999)*.
- UK oil licences (from 1 July 1999).
- Payment entitlement under farmers' single payment scheme (from 22 March 2005).

The 'replacement' assets must be acquired within 12 months before or three years after the disposal of the old asset. Both assets must be within any of the above classes. Holdover relief is available where the new asset is a depreciating asset (having a predictable useful life not exceeding 60 years).

Personal representatives

Allowable expenses
Expenses allowable for the costs of establishing title in computing chargeable gains on disposal of assets in a deceased person's estate: deaths occurring after 5 April 2004 (SP 2/04). (HMRC accepts computations based either on the scale or on the actual allowable expenditure incurred.)

Gross value of estate	Allowable expenditure
Up to £50,000	1.8% of the probate value of the assets sold by the personal representatives
Between £50,001 and £90,000	£900, to be divided between all the assets of the estate in proportion to the probate values and allowed in those proportions on assets sold by the personal representatives
Between £90,001 and £400,000	1% of the probate value of the assets sold
Between £400,001 and £500,000	£4,000, to be divided between all the assets of the estate in proportion to the probate values and allowed in those proportions on assets sold by the personal representatives
Between £500,001 and £1,000,000	0.8% of the probate value of the assets sold
Between £1,000,001 and £5,000,000	£8,000 to be divided between all the assets of the estate in proportion to the probate values and allowed in those proportions on assets sold by the personal representatives
Exceeding £5,000,000	0.16% of the probate value of the assets sold subject to a maximum of £10,000

Trustees

Allowable expenses
Expenses allowable in computing chargeable gains of corporate trustees in the administration of trusts and estates: acquisition, disposals and deemed disposals after 5 April 2004 (SP 2/04). (HMRC accepts computations based either on the scale or on the actual allowable expenditure incurred.)

Transfers of assets to beneficiaries etc	
(a) Quoted stocks and shares	
(i) One beneficiary	£25 per holding
(ii) More than one beneficiary	£25 per holding, divided equally between the beneficiaries
(b) Unquoted shares	As (a) above, plus any exceptional expenditure
(c) Other assets	As (a) above, plus any exceptional expenditure
Actual disposals and acquisitions	
(a) Quoted stocks and shares	Investment fee as charged by the trustees (where a comprehensive annual management fee is charged, the investment fee is taken to be £0.25 per £100 of the sale or purchase moneys)
(b) Unquoted shares	As (a) above, plus actual valuation costs
(c) Other assets	Investment fee (as (a) above), subject to a maximum of £75, plus actual valuation costs
Deemed disposals by trustees	
(a) Quoted stocks and shares	£8 per holding
(b) Unquoted shares	Actual valuation costs
(c) Other assets	Actual valuation costs

Indexation allowance – corporation tax on capital gains

For corporation tax purposes, an indexation allowance is given as a deduction in calculating gains on disposals from the amount realised (or deemed to be realised) on disposal. The indexation allowance is calculated by multiplying each item of allowable expenditure by:

$$\frac{RD - RI}{RI}$$

Where:
  RD is the retail prices index figure for month of disposal;
  RI is the retail prices index for month of expenditure (or March 1982 if later).
See p 26 for indexation allowances up to April 1998 and taper relief which applies thereafter on disposals made after 5 April 1998 by individuals, trustees and personal representatives. See p 44 for RPI values. The factors following can be used to calculate the indexation allowance:

MONTH OF DISPOSAL

	2006											2007			
1982	Feb	Mar	Apr	May	June	July	Aug	Sep	Oct	Nov	Dec	Jan	Feb	Mar	Apr
Mar	1·445	1·455	1·473	1·489	1·499	1·499	1·507	1·519	1·523	1·531	1·552	1·538	1·557	1·573	1·586
Apr	1·396	1·406	1·425	1·440	1·449	1·449	1·458	1·469	1·473	1·482	1·501	1·488	1·506	1·522	1·535
May	1·379	1·389	1·407	1·422	1·432	1·432	1·441	1·452	1·455	1·464	1·483	1·470	1·488	1·504	1·516
June	1·373	1·382	1·401	1·415	1·425	1·425	1·434	1·445	1·448	1·457	1·476	1·463	1·481	1·497	1·509
July	1·372	1·382	1·400	1·415	1·424	1·424	1·433	1·444	1·448	1·456	1·476	1·462	1·481	1·496	1·509
Aug	1·371	1·381	1·399	1·414	1·424	1·424	1·432	1·443	1·447	1·455	1·475	1·462	1·480	1·496	1·508
Sept	1·373	1·382	1·401	1·415	1·425	1·425	1·434	1·445	1·448	1·457	1·476	1·463	1·481	1·497	1·509
Oct	1·361	1·371	1·389	1·403	1·413	1·413	1·422	1·433	1·436	1·445	1·464	1·451	1·469	1·485	1·497
Nov	1·349	1·359	1·377	1·392	1·401	1·401	1·410	1·421	1·424	1·433	1·452	1·439	1·457	1·473	1·485
Dec	1·354	1·363	1·382	1·396	1·406	1·406	1·414	1·425	1·429	1·437	1·457	1·443	1·462	1·477	1·489
1983	Feb	Mar	Apr	May	June	July	Aug	Sep	Oct	Nov	Dec	Jan	Feb	Mar	Apr
Jan	1·351	1·360	1·379	1·393	1·403	1·403	1·411	1·422	1·426	1·434	1·454	1·440	1·459	1·474	1·486
Feb	1·341	1·350	1·368	1·383	1·393	1·393	1·401	1·412	1·415	1·424	1·443	1·430	1·448	1·464	1·476
Mar	1·336	1·346	1·364	1·379	1·388	1·388	1·397	1·407	1·411	1·419	1·439	1·425	1·444	1·459	1·471
Apr	1·304	1·314	1·331	1·346	1·355	1·355	1·363	1·374	1·378	1·386	1·405	1·392	1·410	1·425	1·437
May	1·294	1·304	1·322	1·336	1·345	1·345	1·354	1·364	1·368	1·376	1·395	1·382	1·400	1·415	1·427
June	1·289	1·298	1·316	1·330	1·340	1·340	1·348	1·359	1·362	1·370	1·389	1·376	1·394	1·409	1·421
July	1·277	1·286	1·304	1·318	1·327	1·327	1·335	1·346	1·349	1·358	1·376	1·363	1·381	1·396	1·408
Aug	1·267	1·276	1·293	1·307	1·317	1·317	1·325	1·335	1·339	1·347	1·366	1·353	1·371	1·386	1·397
Sept	1·257	1·266	1·283	1·297	1·307	1·307	1·315	1·325	1·329	1·337	1·355	1·343	1·360	1·375	1·387
Oct	1·249	1·258	1·275	1·289	1·298	1·298	1·307	1·317	1·320	1·329	1·347	1·334	1·352	1·367	1·378
Nov	1·241	1·250	1·267	1·281	1·290	1·290	1·298	1·309	1·312	1·320	1·339	1·326	1·343	1·358	1·370
Dec	1·235	1·244	1·261	1·275	1·284	1·284	1·292	1·303	1·306	1·314	1·333	1·320	1·337	1·352	1·364
1984	Feb	Mar	Apr	May	June	July	Aug	Sep	Oct	Nov	Dec	Jan	Feb	Mar	Apr
Jan	1·236	1·245	1·263	1·276	1·286	1·286	1·294	1·304	1·308	1·316	1·334	1·321	1·339	1·354	1·365
Feb	1·227	1·236	1·253	1·267	1·276	1·276	1·284	1·295	1·298	1·306	1·325	1·312	1·329	1·344	1·356
Mar	1·220	1·229	1·246	1·260	1·269	1·269	1·277	1·287	1·291	1·299	1·317	1·305	1·322	1·337	1·348
Apr	1·191	1·200	1·217	1·230	1·239	1·239	1·247	1·257	1·261	1·269	1·287	1·274	1·291	1·306	1·317
May	1·183	1·192	1·209	1·222	1·231	1·231	1·239	1·249	1·252	1·260	1·278	1·266	1·283	1·297	1·309
June	1·177	1·186	1·203	1·216	1·225	1·225	1·233	1·243	1·247	1·254	1·272	1·260	1·277	1·291	1·303
July	1·180	1·189	1·205	1·219	1·228	1·228	1·236	1·246	1·249	1·257	1·275	1·263	1·279	1·294	1·305
Aug	1·159	1·168	1·185	1·198	1·207	1·207	1·215	1·225	1·228	1·236	1·254	1·242	1·258	1·273	1·284
Sept	1·155	1·164	1·181	1·194	1·203	1·203	1·211	1·221	1·224	1·232	1·249	1·237	1·254	1·268	1·279
Oct	1·142	1·151	1·167	1·180	1·189	1·189	1·197	1·207	1·210	1·218	1·236	1·223	1·240	1·254	1·265
Nov	1·135	1·144	1·161	1·174	1·183	1·183	1·190	1·200	1·203	1·211	1·229	1·217	1·233	1·247	1·258
Dec	1·137	1·146	1·162	1·176	1·184	1·184	1·192	1·202	1·205	1·213	1·231	1·218	1·235	1·249	1·260
1985	Feb	Mar	Apr	May	June	July	Aug	Sep	Oct	Nov	Dec	Jan	Feb	Mar	Apr
Jan	1·129	1·138	1·155	1·168	1·176	1·176	1·184	1·194	1·197	1·205	1·222	1·210	1·227	1·241	1·252
Feb	1·112	1·121	1·137	1·150	1·159	1·159	1·167	1·176	1·180	1·187	1·205	1·193	1·209	1·223	1·234
Mar	1·093	1·101	1·117	1·130	1·139	1·139	1·147	1·156	1·159	1·167	1·184	1·172	1·189	1·203	1·213
Apr	1·049	1·057	1·073	1·086	1·094	1·094	1·102	1·111	1·114	1·122	1·139	1·127	1·143	1·157	1·167
May	1·040	1·048	1·064	1·076	1·085	1·085	1·092	1·102	1·105	1·112	1·129	1·117	1·133	1·147	1·157
June	1·035	1·044	1·059	1·072	1·080	1·080	1·088	1·097	1·100	1·108	1·124	1·113	1·129	1·142	1·153
July	1·039	1·048	1·063	1·076	1·084	1·084	1·092	1·101	1·104	1·112	1·128	1·117	1·133	1·146	1·157
Aug	1·034	1·042	1·058	1·070	1·079	1·079	1·086	1·096	1·099	1·106	1·123	1·111	1·127	1·141	1·151
Sept	1·035	1·043	1·059	1·072	1·080	1·080	1·087	1·097	1·100	1·107	1·124	1·112	1·128	1·142	1·152
Oct	1·032	1·040	1·056	1·068	1·077	1·077	1·084	1·093	1·096	1·104	1·121	1·109	1·125	1·138	1·149
Nov	1·025	1·033	1·049	1·061	1·069	1·069	1·077	1·086	1·089	1·097	1·113	1·102	1·117	1·131	1·141
Dec	1·022	1·030	1·046	1·058	1·067	1·067	1·074	1·083	1·087	1·094	1·110	1·099	1·115	1·128	1·139

MONTH OF DISPOSAL

	2007								2008						
1982	May	June	July	Aug	Sep	Oct	Nov	Dec	Jan	Feb	Mar	Apr	May	June	July
Mar	1·596	1·609	1·594	1·609	1·618	1·630	1·640	1·655	1·641	1·661	1·670	1·694	1·708	1·729	1·725
Apr	1·544	1·558	1·543	1·558	1·567	1·578	1·588	1·602	1·589	1·609	1·617	1·641	1·654	1·675	1·672
May	1·526	1·540	1·525	1·540	1·548	1·559	1·569	1·584	1·570	1·590	1·599	1·622	1·635	1·656	1·652
June	1·519	1·533	1·518	1·533	1·541	1·552	1·562	1·577	1·563	1·583	1·591	1·615	1·628	1·649	1·645
July	1·518	1·532	1·517	1·532	1·540	1·551	1·561	1·576	1·562	1·582	1·591	1·614	1·627	1·648	1·648
Aug	1·518	1·531	1·516	1·531	1·540	1·551	1·560	1·575	1·562	1·581	1·590	1·613	1·626	1·647	1·647
Sept	1·519	1·533	1·518	1·533	1·541	1·552	1·562	1·577	1·563	1·583	1·591	1·615	1·628	1·649	1·645
Oct	1·507	1·520	1·506	1·520	1·529	1·540	1·549	1·564	1·551	1·570	1·579	1·602	1·615	1·636	1·632
Nov	1·495	1·508	1·493	1·508	1·516	1·527	1·537	1·551	1·538	1·557	1·566	1·589	1·602	1·623	1·619
Dec	1·499	1·512	1·498	1·512	1·521	1·532	1·542	1·556	1·543	1·562	1·571	1·594	1·607	1·628	1·624
1983	May	June	July	Aug	Sep	Oct	Nov	Dec	Jan	Feb	Mar	Apr	May	June	July
Jan	1·496	1·509	1·495	1·509	1·518	1·529	1·538	1·553	1·540	1·559	1·567	1·590	1·604	1·624	1·621
Feb	1·485	1·499	1·484	1·499	1·507	1·518	1·528	1·542	1·529	1·548	1·556	1·579	1·593	1·613	1·610
Mar	1·481	1·494	1·480	1·494	1·502	1·513	1·523	1·537	1·524	1·543	1·552	1·575	1·588	1·608	1·605
Apr	1·446	1·460	1·445	1·460	1·468	1·479	1·488	1·502	1·489	1·508	1·516	1·539	1·552	1·572	1·569
May	1·436	1·449	1·435	1·449	1·458	1·468	1·478	1·492	1·479	1·498	1·506	1·528	1·541	1·561	1·558
June	1·430	1·443	1·429	1·443	1·452	1·462	1·472	1·486	1·473	1·492	1·500	1·522	1·535	1·555	1·552
July	1·417	1·430	1·416	1·430	1·439	1·449	1·458	1·473	1·460	1·478	1·487	1·509	1·522	1·542	1·542
Aug	1·407	1·420	1·406	1·420	1·428	1·438	1·448	1·462	1·449	1·467	1·476	1·498	1·511	1·530	1·530
Sept	1·396	1·409	1·395	1·409	1·417	1·427	1·437	1·451	1·438	1·456	1·465	1·487	1·499	1·519	1·516
Oct	1·388	1·400	1·386	1·400	1·408	1·419	1·428	1·442	1·429	1·448	1·456	1·478	1·491	1·510	1·507
Nov	1·379	1·392	1·378	1·392	1·400	1·410	1·420	1·433	1·421	1·469	1·447	1·469	1·482	1·502	1·498
Dec	1·373	1·386	1·372	1·386	1·394	1·404	1·413	1·427	1·414	1·433	1·441	1·463	1·475	1·495	1·492
1984	May	June	July	Aug	Sep	Oct	Nov	Dec	Jan	Feb	Mar	Apr	May	June	July
Jan	1·374	1·387	1·373	1·387	1·395	1·405	1·415	1·428	1·416	1·434	1·442	1·464	1·477	1·496	1·493
Feb	1·365	1·377	1·364	1·377	1·385	1·396	1·405	1·419	1·406	1·424	1·432	1·454	1·467	1·486	1·483
Mar	1·357	1·370	1·356	1·370	1·378	1·388	1·397	1·411	1·398	1·417	1·425	1·446	1·459	1·478	1·475
Apr	1·326	1·339	1·325	1·339	1·346	1·357	1·366	1·379	1·367	1·385	1·393	1·414	1·427	1·446	1·442
May	1·318	1·330	1·316	1·330	1·338	1·348	1·357	1·370	1·358	1·376	1·384	1·405	1·418	1·437	1·433
June	1·312	1·324	1·310	1·324	1·332	1·342	1·351	1·364	1·352	1·370	1·378	1·399	1·411	1·430	1·427
July	1·314	1·327	1·313	1·327	1·334	1·345	1·354	1·367	1·355	1·373	1·380	1·402	1·414	1·433	1·433
Aug	1·293	1·305	1·292	1·305	1·313	1·323	1·332	1·345	1·333	1·351	1·358	1·379	1·392	1·411	1·411
Sept	1·288	1·300	1·287	1·300	1·308	1·318	1·327	1·340	1·328	1·346	1·354	1·375	1·387	1·406	1·403
Oct	1·274	1·286	1·273	1·286	1·294	1·304	1·313	1·326	1·314	1·331	1·339	1·360	1·372	1·391	1·388
Nov	1·267	1·279	1·266	1·279	1·287	1·297	1·306	1·319	1·307	1·324	1·332	1·353	1·365	1·384	1·380
Dec	1·269	1·281	1·268	1·281	1·289	1·299	1·308	1·321	1·309	1·326	1·334	1·355	1·367	1·386	1·382
1985	May	June	July	Aug	Sep	Oct	Nov	Dec	Jan	Feb	Mar	Apr	May	June	July
Jan	1·261	1·273	1·260	1·273	1·281	1·290	1·299	1·312	1·300	1·318	1·326	1·346	1·358	1·377	1·374
Feb	1·243	1·255	1·242	1·255	1·262	1·272	1·281	1·294	1·282	1·299	1·307	1·328	1·340	1·358	1·355
Mar	1·222	1·234	1·221	1·234	1·241	1·251	1·260	1·273	1·261	1·278	1·286	1·306	1·318	1·336	1·333
Apr	1·176	1·187	1·175	1·187	1·195	1·204	1·213	1·225	1·214	1·230	1·238	1·258	1·270	1·287	1·284
May	1·166	1·177	1·165	1·177	1·185	1·194	1·203	1·215	1·204	1·220	1·228	1·248	1·259	1·277	1·274
June	1·161	1·173	1·160	1·173	1·180	1·189	1·198	1·210	1·199	1·216	1·223	1·243	1·254	1·272	1·269
July	1·165	1·177	1·164	1·177	1·184	1·194	1·202	1·215	1·203	1·220	1·227	1·247	1·259	1·276	1·276
Aug	1·159	1·171	1·158	1·171	1·178	1·188	1·196	1·209	1·197	1·214	1·221	1·241	1·253	1·270	1·270
Sept	1·161	1·172	1·160	1·172	1·179	1·189	1·197	1·210	1·198	1·215	1·222	1·242	1·254	1·272	1·269
Oct	1·157	1·169	1·156	1·169	1·176	1·185	1·194	1·206	1·195	1·212	1·219	1·239	1·250	1·268	1·265
Nov	1·150	1·161	1·149	1·161	1·168	1·178	1·186	1·199	1·187	1·204	1·211	1·231	1·243	1·260	1·257
Dec	1·147	1·158	1·146	1·158	1·166	1·175	1·183	1·196	1·184	1·201	1·208	1·228	1·240	1·257	1·254

MONTH OF DISPOSAL

	2006											2007			
1986	Feb	Mar	Apr	May	June	July	Aug	Sep	Oct	Nov	Dec	Jan	Feb	Mar	Apr
Jan	1·018	1·026	1·042	1·054	1·062	1·062	1·070	1·079	1·082	1·089	1·106	1·095	1·110	1·124	1·134
Feb	1·010	1·019	1·034	1·047	1·055	1·055	1·062	1·071	1·074	1·082	1·098	1·087	1·102	1·116	1·126
Mar	1·008	1·016	1·031	1·044	1·052	1·052	1·059	1·069	1·072	1·079	1·096	1·084	1·100	1·113	1·123
Apr	·988	·997	1·012	1·024	1·032	1·032	1·040	1·049	1·052	1·059	1·075	1·064	1·079	1·093	1·103
May	·985	·993	1·008	1·021	1·029	1·029	1·036	1·045	1·048	1·055	1·072	1·060	1·076	1·089	1·099
June	·986	·994	1·009	1·022	1·030	1·030	1·037	1·046	1·049	1·056	1·073	1·061	1·077	1·090	1·100
July	·991	1·000	1·015	1·027	1·036	1·036	1·043	1·052	1·055	1·062	1·079	1·067	1·083	1·096	1·106
Aug	·985	·993	1·009	1·021	1·029	1·029	1·036	1·046	1·049	1·056	1·072	1·061	1·076	1·090	1·100
Sept	·976	·984	·999	1·011	1·019	1·019	1·026	1·036	1·039	1·046	1·062	1·051	1·066	1·079	1·089
Oct	·973	·981	·996	1·008	1·016	1·016	1·023	1·032	1·035	1·043	1·059	1·048	1·063	1·076	1·086
Nov	·956	·964	·979	·991	·999	·999	1·006	1·015	1·018	1·025	1·041	1·030	1·046	1·059	1·069
Dec	·949	·957	·973	·985	·993	·993	1·000	1·009	1·012	1·019	1·035	1·024	1·039	1·052	1·062
1987	Feb	Mar	Apr	May	June	July	Aug	Sep	Oct	Nov	Dec	Jan	Feb	Mar	Apr
Jan	·942	·950	·965	·977	·985	·985	·992	1·001	1·004	1·011	1·027	1·016	1·031	1·044	1·054
Feb	·934	·942	·957	·969	·977	·977	·984	·993	·996	1·003	1·019	1·008	1·023	1·036	1·046
Mar	·930	·938	·953	·965	·973	·973	·980	·989	·992	·999	1·015	1·004	1·019	1·032	1·042
Apr	·908	·916	·930	·942	·950	·950	·957	·966	·969	·975	·991	·980	·995	1·008	1·018
May	·906	·914	·928	·940	·948	·948	·955	·964	·967	·974	·989	·978	·993	1·006	1·016
June	·906	·914	·928	·940	·948	·948	·955	·964	·967	·974	·989	·978	·993	1·006	1·016
July	·908	·916	·930	·942	·950	·950	·957	·966	·969	·975	·991	·980	·995	1·008	1·018
Aug	·902	·910	·925	·936	·944	·944	·951	·960	·963	·970	·985	·975	·989	1·002	1·012
Sept	·896	·904	·919	·931	·938	·938	·945	·954	·957	·964	·979	·969	·983	·996	1·006
Oct	·887	·895	·910	·921	·929	·929	·936	·945	·948	·954	·970	·959	·974	·986	·996
Nov	·878	·886	·900	·912	·920	·920	·926	·935	·938	·945	·960	·950	·964	·977	·986
Dec	·880	·888	·902	·914	·922	·922	·928	·937	·940	·947	·962	·952	·966	·979	·988
1988	Feb	Mar	Apr	May	June	July	Aug	Sep	Oct	Nov	Dec	Jan	Feb	Mar	Apr
Jan	·880	·888	·902	·914	·922	·922	·928	·937	·940	·947	·962	·952	·966	·979	·988
Feb	·873	·880	·895	·906	·914	·914	·921	·930	·932	·939	·955	·944	·959	·971	·981
Mar	·866	·873	·888	·899	·907	·907	·914	·922	·925	·932	·947	·937	·951	·963	·973
Apr	·836	·843	·857	·869	·876	·876	·883	·891	·894	·901	·916	·905	·920	·932	·941
May	·829	·836	·850	·862	·869	·869	·876	·884	·887	·894	·909	·898	·912	·925	·934
June	·822	·829	·843	·855	·862	·862	·869	·877	·880	·886	·902	·891	·905	·917	·927
July	·820	·828	·842	·853	·860	·860	·867	·875	·878	·885	·900	·889	·903	·916	·925
Aug	·800	·807	·821	·832	·840	·840	·846	·854	·857	·864	·879	·868	·882	·894	·904
Sept	·792	·799	·813	·824	·831	·831	·838	·846	·849	·855	·870	·860	·874	·886	·895
Oct	·774	·781	·795	·805	·813	·813	·819	·827	·830	·837	·851	·841	·855	·867	·876
Nov	·765	·773	·786	·797	·805	·805	·811	·819	·822	·828	·843	·833	·846	·858	·867
Dec	·761	·768	·782	·792	·800	·800	·806	·814	·817	·823	·838	·828	·841	·853	·862
1989	Feb	Mar	Apr	May	June	July	Aug	Sep	Oct	Nov	Dec	Jan	Feb	Mar	Apr
Jan	·750	·757	·770	·781	·788	·788	·795	·803	·805	·812	·826	·816	·830	·841	·850
Feb	·737	·744	·758	·768	·775	·775	·782	·790	·792	·799	·813	·803	·817	·828	·837
Mar	·729	·736	·750	·760	·768	·768	·774	·782	·785	·791	·805	·795	·809	·820	·829
Apr	·699	·706	·719	·730	·737	·737	·743	·751	·753	·759	·773	·764	·777	·788	·797
May	·689	·696	·709	·719	·726	·726	·732	·740	·743	·749	·763	·753	·766	·777	·786
June	·683	·690	·703	·713	·720	·720	·726	·734	·737	·743	·756	·747	·760	·771	·780
July	·681	·688	·701	·712	·719	·719	·725	·732	·735	·741	·755	·745	·758	·770	·778
Aug	·677	·684	·697	·707	·714	·714	·720	·728	·731	·737	·750	·741	·754	·765	·774
Sept	·666	·672	·685	·696	·702	·702	·708	·716	·719	·725	·738	·729	·742	·753	·762
Oct	·653	·660	·672	·683	·689	·689	·695	·703	·706	·711	·725	·716	·729	·740	·748
Nov	·639	·646	·658	·668	·675	·675	·681	·689	·691	·697	·711	·701	·714	·725	·733
Dec	·635	·641	·654	·664	·671	·671	·677	·684	·687	·693	·706	·697	·710	·721	·729

MONTH OF DISPOSAL

	2007								2008						
1986	May	June	July	Aug	Sep	Oct	Nov	Dec	Jan	Feb	Mar	Apr	May	June	July
Jan	1·142	1·154	1·141	1·154	1·161	1·170	1·179	1·191	1·180	1·196	1·204	1·223	1·235	1·253	1·249
Feb	1·135	1·146	1·133	1·146	1·153	1·162	1·171	1·183	1·172	1·188	1·196	1·215	1·227	1·244	1·241
Mar	1·132	1·143	1·131	1·143	1·150	1·160	1·168	1·180	1·169	1·185	1·193	1·212	1·224	1·241	1·238
Apr	1·111	1·122	1·110	1·122	1·130	1·139	1·147	1·159	1·148	1·164	1·172	1·191	1·202	1·220	1·217
May	1·107	1·119	1·106	1·119	1·126	1·135	1·143	1·155	1·144	1·161	1·168	1·187	1·198	1·216	1·213
June	1·108	1·120	1·107	1·120	1·127	1·136	1·144	1·157	1·145	1·162	1·169	1·188	1·200	1·217	1·214
July	1·115	1·126	1·114	1·126	1·133	1·142	1·150	1·163	1·151	1·168	1·175	1·195	1·206	1·223	1·223
Aug	1·108	1·119	1·107	1·119	1·126	1·136	1·144	1·156	1·145	1·161	1·168	1·188	1·199	1·216	1·216
Sept	1·098	1·109	1·097	1·109	1·116	1·125	1·133	1·145	1·134	1·151	1·158	1·177	1·188	1·205	1·202
Oct	1·094	1·106	1·093	1·106	1·113	1·122	1·130	1·142	1·131	1·147	1·154	1·174	1·185	1·202	1·199
Nov	1·077	1·088	1·076	1·088	1·095	1·104	1·112	1·124	1·113	1·129	1·136	1·155	1·166	1·183	1·180
Dec	1·070	1·081	1·069	1·081	1·088	1·097	1·105	1·117	1·106	1·122	1·129	1·148	1·159	1·176	1·173
1987	May	June	July	Aug	Sep	Oct	Nov	Dec	Jan	Feb	Mar	Apr	May	June	July
Jan	1·062	1·073	1·061	1·073	1·080	1·089	1·097	1·109	1·098	1·114	1·121	1·140	1·151	1·168	1·165
Feb	1·054	1·065	1·053	1·065	1·072	1·081	1·089	1·101	1·090	1·106	1·113	1·131	1·142	1·159	1·156
Mar	1·050	1·061	1·049	1·061	1·068	1·077	1·084	1·096	1·085	1·101	1·108	1·127	1·138	1·155	1·152
Apr	1·026	1·036	1·025	1·036	1·043	1·052	1·060	1·072	1·061	1·077	1·083	1·102	1·113	1·130	1·127
May	1·024	1·034	1·023	1·034	1·041	1·050	1·058	1·070	1·059	1·075	1·081	1·100	1·111	1·128	1·125
June	1·024	1·034	1·023	1·034	1·041	1·050	1·058	1·070	1·059	1·075	1·081	1·100	1·111	1·128	1·125
July	1·026	1·036	1·025	1·036	1·043	1·052	1·060	1·072	1·061	1·077	1·083	1·102	1·113	1·130	1·130
Aug	1·020	1·030	1·019	1·030	1·037	1·046	1·054	1·066	1·055	1·071	1·077	1·096	1·107	1·123	1·123
Sept	1·014	1·024	1·013	1·024	1·031	1·040	1·048	1·060	1·049	1·064	1·071	1·090	1·101	1·117	1·114
Oct	1·004	1·015	1·003	1·015	1·021	1·030	1·038	1·050	1·039	1·054	1·061	1·080	1·090	1·107	1·104
Nov	·994	1·005	·993	1·005	1·012	1·020	1·028	1·040	1·029	1·044	1·051	1·070	1·080	1·097	1·094
Dec	·996	1·007	·995	1·007	1·014	1·022	1·030	1·042	1·031	1·046	1·053	1·072	1·082	1·099	1·096
1988	May	June	July	Aug	Sep	Oct	Nov	Dec	Jan	Feb	Mar	Apr	May	June	July
Jan	·996	1·007	·995	1·007	1·014	1·022	1·030	1·042	1·031	1·046	1·053	1·072	1·082	1·099	1·096
Feb	·988	·999	·987	·999	1·006	1·014	1·022	1·034	1·023	1·039	1·045	1·064	1·074	1·091	1·088
Mar	·981	·991	·980	·991	·998	1·007	1·014	1·026	1·015	1·031	1·037	1·056	1·066	1·083	1·080
Apr	·949	·959	·948	·959	·966	·974	·982	·993	·983	·998	1·005	1·023	1·033	1·049	1·046
May	·942	·952	·941	·952	·959	·967	·975	·986	·976	·991	·997	1·015	1·025	1·041	1·039
June	·934	·945	·933	·945	·951	·960	·967	·978	·968	·983	·990	1·008	1·018	1·034	1·031
July	·933	·943	·932	·943	·949	·958	·965	·977	·966	·981	·988	1·006	1·016	1·032	1·032
Aug	·911	·921	·910	·921	·928	·936	·943	·955	·944	·959	·966	·983	·994	1·009	1·009
Sept	·902	·912	·901	·912	·919	·927	·935	·946	·935	·950	·957	·974	·984	1·000	·997
Oct	·883	·893	·882	·893	·900	·908	·915	·926	·916	·931	·937	·954	·964	·980	·977
Nov	·875	·885	·874	·885	·891	·899	·906	·917	·907	·922	·928	·945	·955	·971	·968
Dec	·869	·879	·869	·879	·886	·894	·901	·912	·902	·917	·923	·940	·950	·966	·963
1989	May	June	July	Aug	Sep	Oct	Nov	Dec	Jan	Feb	Mar	Apr	May	June	July
Jan	·858	·868	·857	·868	·874	·882	·889	·900	·890	·905	·911	·928	·938	·953	·950
Feb	·844	·854	·843	·854	·860	·869	·876	·886	·877	·891	·897	·914	·924	·939	·936
Mar	·836	·846	·835	·846	·852	·860	·867	·878	·868	·882	·889	·906	·915	·931	·928
Apr	·804	·814	·803	·814	·820	·828	·835	·845	·836	·850	·856	·872	·882	·897	·894
May	·793	·803	·792	·803	·809	·817	·823	·834	·824	·838	·844	·861	·870	·885	·883
June	·787	·796	·786	·796	·802	·810	·817	·828	·818	·832	·838	·854	·864	·879	·876
July	·785	·795	·784	·795	·801	·809	·816	·826	·816	·830	·836	·853	·862	·877	·874
Aug	·781	·790	·780	·790	·796	·804	·811	·821	·812	·826	·832	·848	·858	·872	·870
Sept	·768	·778	·768	·778	·784	·792	·798	·809	·799	·813	·819	·835	·845	·859	·857
Oct	·755	·764	·754	·764	·770	·778	·785	·795	·786	·799	·805	·821	·831	·845	·843
Nov	·740	·749	·739	·749	·755	·763	·770	·780	·770	·784	·790	·806	·815	·830	·827
Dec	·736	·745	·735	·745	·751	·758	·765	·775	·766	·779	·785	·801	·811	·825	·822

MONTH OF DISPOSAL

1990	Feb	Mar	Apr	May	June	July	Aug	Sep	Oct	Nov	Dec	Jan	Feb	Mar	Apr
					2006							2007			
Jan	·625	·632	·644	·654	·661	·661	·667	·674	·677	·683	·696	·687	·700	·710	·719
Feb	·616	·622	·635	·645	·651	·651	·657	·665	·667	·673	·686	·677	·690	·700	·709
Mar	·600	·606	·619	·629	·635	·635	·641	·648	·651	·657	·670	·661	·673	·684	·692
Apr	·552	·559	·571	·580	·587	·587	·592	·600	·602	·608	·620	·612	·624	·634	·642
May	·539	·545	·557	·567	·573	·573	·578	·586	·588	·594	·606	·597	·609	·620	·628
June	·533	·539	·551	·560	·567	·567	·572	·579	·582	·587	·600	·591	·603	·613	·621
July	·532	·538	·550	·559	·565	·565	·571	·578	·580	·586	·599	·590	·602	·612	·620
Aug	·516	·522	·534	·543	·550	·550	·555	·562	·564	·570	·582	·574	·585	·596	·603
Sept	·502	·508	·520	·529	·535	·535	·541	·548	·550	·555	·568	·559	·571	·581	·589
Oct	·490	·497	·508	·517	·523	·523	·529	·536	·538	·543	·556	·547	·559	·569	·576
Nov	·494	·500	·512	·521	·527	·527	·532	·539	·542	·547	·559	·551	·562	·572	·580
Dec	·495	·501	·513	·522	·528	·528	·533	·540	·543	·548	·560	·552	·564	·574	·581
1991	Feb	Mar	Apr	May	June	July	Aug	Sep	Oct	Nov	Dec	Jan	Feb	Mar	Apr
Jan	·492	·498	·509	·518	·525	·525	·530	·537	·539	·545	·557	·548	·560	·570	·578
Feb	·484	·490	·501	·510	·516	·516	·522	·529	·531	·536	·549	·540	·552	·561	·569
Mar	·478	·484	·495	·505	·511	·511	·516	·523	·525	·530	·543	·534	·546	·556	·563
Apr	·459	·465	·476	·485	·491	·491	·497	·503	·506	·511	·523	·515	·526	·536	·543
May	·455	·461	·472	·481	·487	·487	·492	·499	·501	·506	·518	·510	·521	·531	·539
June	·448	·454	·465	·474	·480	·480	·485	·492	·494	·500	·512	·503	·515	·524	·532
July	·451	·457	·469	·478	·484	·484	·489	·496	·498	·503	·515	·507	·518	·528	·535
Aug	·448	·454	·465	·474	·480	·480	·485	·492	·494	·500	·512	·503	·515	·524	·532
Sept	·443	·449	·460	·469	·475	·475	·480	·487	·489	·494	·506	·498	·509	·519	·526
Oct	·437	·443	·454	·463	·469	·469	·474	·481	·483	·489	·500	·492	·503	·513	·520
Nov	·432	·438	·449	·458	·464	·464	·469	·476	·478	·483	·495	·487	·498	·507	·515
Dec	·431	·437	·448	·457	·463	·463	·468	·475	·477	·482	·494	·486	·497	·506	·514
1992	Feb	Mar	Apr	May	June	July	Aug	Sep	Oct	Nov	Dec	Jan	Feb	Mar	Apr
Jan	·432	·438	·449	·458	·464	·464	·469	·476	·478	·483	·495	·487	·498	·507	·515
Feb	·425	·431	·442	·450	·456	·456	·461	·468	·470	·475	·487	·479	·490	·500	·507
Mar	·421	·426	·437	·446	·452	·452	·457	·464	·466	·471	·483	·475	·486	·495	·503
Apr	·399	·405	·416	·424	·430	·430	·435	·442	·444	·449	·460	·452	·463	·473	·480
May	·394	·400	·411	·419	·425	·425	·430	·436	·439	·444	·455	·447	·458	·467	·475
June	·394	·400	·411	·419	·425	·425	·430	·436	·439	·444	·455	·447	·458	·467	·475
July	·399	·405	·416	·424	·430	·430	·435	·442	·444	·449	·460	·452	·463	·473	·480
Aug	·398	·404	·415	·423	·429	·429	·434	·441	·443	·448	·459	·451	·462	·472	·479
Sept	·393	·399	·410	·418	·424	·424	·429	·435	·438	·443	·454	·446	·457	·466	·473
Oct	·388	·394	·405	·413	·419	·419	·424	·430	·432	·437	·449	·441	·452	·461	·468
Nov	·390	·396	·407	·415	·421	·421	·426	·432	·435	·440	·451	·443	·454	·463	·470
Dec	·395	·401	·412	·420	·426	·426	·431	·438	·440	·445	·456	·448	·459	·468	·476
1993	Feb	Mar	Apr	May	June	July	Aug	Sep	Oct	Nov	Dec	Jan	Feb	Mar	Apr
Jan	·408	·414	·425	·434	·439	·439	·445	·451	·453	·458	·470	·462	·473	·482	·489
Feb	·399	·405	·416	·424	·430	·430	·435	·442	·444	·449	·460	·452	·463	·473	·480
Mar	·394	·400	·411	·419	·425	·425	·430	·436	·439	·444	·455	·447	·458	·467	·475
Apr	·381	·387	·398	·406	·412	·412	·417	·423	·425	·430	·442	·434	·445	·454	·461
May	·376	·382	·393	·401	·407	·407	·412	·418	·420	·425	·437	·429	·439	·449	·456
June	·377	·383	·394	·402	·408	·408	·413	·419	·421	·426	·438	·430	·440	·450	·457
July	·380	·386	·397	·405	·411	·411	·416	·422	·424	·429	·441	·433	·443	·453	·460
Aug	·374	·380	·391	·399	·405	·405	·410	·416	·418	·423	·435	·427	·437	·447	·454
Sept	·369	·374	·385	·393	·399	·399	·404	·410	·412	·417	·428	·421	·431	·440	·447
Oct	·370	·375	·386	·394	·400	·400	·405	·411	·413	·418	·429	·422	·432	·441	·449
Nov	·371	·377	·388	·396	·402	·402	·407	·413	·415	·420	·431	·424	·434	·444	·451
Dec	·369	·374	·385	·393	·399	·399	·404	·410	·412	·417	·428	·421	·431	·440	·447

MONTH OF DISPOSAL

	2007								2008						
1990	May	June	July	Aug	Sep	Oct	Nov	Dec	Jan	Feb	Mar	Apr	May	June	July
Jan	·726	·735	·725	·735	·741	·748	·755	·765	·756	·769	·775	·791	·800	·814	·812
Feb	·715	·725	·715	·725	·730	·738	·745	·755	·745	·759	·765	·780	·790	·804	·801
Mar	·699	·708	·698	·708	·713	·721	·727	·737	·728	·741	·747	·763	·772	·786	·783
Apr	·648	·657	·647	·657	·663	·670	·676	·686	·677	·690	·695	·711	·719	·733	·731
May	·634	·643	·633	·643	·648	·655	·662	·671	·662	·675	·681	·696	·704	·718	·716
June	·627	·636	·627	·636	·642	·649	·655	·665	·656	·669	·674	·689	·698	·711	·709
July	·626	·635	·625	·635	·640	·647	·654	·663	·655	·667	·673	·688	·696	·710	·707
Aug	·610	·618	·609	·618	·624	·631	·637	·646	·638	·650	·656	·671	·679	·692	·690
Sept	·595	·603	·594	·603	·609	·616	·622	·631	·623	·635	·640	·655	·664	·677	·674
Oct	·583	·591	·582	·591	·596	·603	·609	·619	·610	·622	·628	·642	·651	·664	·662
Nov	·586	·595	·585	·595	·600	·607	·613	·622	·614	·626	·632	·646	·655	·668	·664
Dec	·587	·596	·587	·596	·601	·608	·614	·624	·615	·627	·633	·647	·656	·669	·667
1991	May	June	July	Aug	Sep	Oct	Nov	Dec	Jan	Feb	Mar	Apr	May	June	July
Jan	·584	·592	·583	·592	·598	·604	·611	·620	·611	·624	·629	·644	·652	·665	·663
Feb	·575	·584	·574	·584	·589	·596	·602	·611	·603	·615	·620	·635	·643	·656	·654
Mar	·569	·578	·568	·578	·583	·590	·596	·605	·597	·609	·614	·629	·637	·650	·648
Apr	·549	·557	·548	·557	·563	·569	·576	·585	·576	·588	·594	·608	·616	·629	·627
May	·545	·553	·544	·553	·558	·565	·571	·580	·572	·584	·589	·603	·611	·624	·622
June	·538	·546	·537	·546	·551	·558	·564	·573	·565	·576	·582	·596	·604	·617	·614
July	·541	·549	·540	·549	·555	·561	·567	·576	·568	·580	·585	·599	·608	·620	·618
Aug	·538	·546	·537	·546	·551	·558	·564	·573	·565	·576	·582	·596	·604	·617	·614
Sept	·532	·540	·531	·540	·545	·552	·558	·567	·559	·571	·576	·590	·598	·611	·608
Oct	·526	·534	·526	·534	·540	·546	·552	·561	·553	·565	·570	·584	·592	·605	·603
Nov	·521	·529	·520	·529	·534	·541	·546	·555	·547	·559	·564	·578	·586	·599	·597
Dec	·520	·528	·519	·528	·533	·539	·545	·554	·546	·558	·563	·577	·585	·598	·595
1992	May	June	July	Aug	Sep	Oct	Nov	Dec	Jan	Feb	Mar	Apr	May	June	July
Jan	·521	·529	·520	·529	·534	·541	·546	·555	·547	·559	·564	·578	·586	·599	·597
Feb	·513	·521	·512	·521	·526	·533	·539	·547	·539	·551	·556	·570	·578	·591	·855
Mar	·508	·516	·508	·516	·522	·528	·534	·543	·535	·546	·552	·565	·574	·586	·584
Apr	·486	·494	·485	·494	·499	·505	·511	·519	·512	·523	·528	·542	·550	·562	·560
May	·480	·488	·480	·488	·493	·500	·505	·514	·506	·518	·523	·536	·544	·556	·554
June	·480	·488	·480	·488	·493	·500	·505	·514	·506	·518	·523	·536	·544	·556	·554
July	·486	·494	·485	·494	·499	·505	·511	·519	·512	·523	·528	·542	·550	·562	·560
Aug	·485	·492	·484	·492	·497	·504	·510	·518	·510	·522	·527	·541	·549	·561	·559
Sept	·479	·487	·478	·487	·492	·499	·504	·513	·505	·516	·522	·535	·543	·555	·553
Oct	·474	·482	·473	·482	·488	·493	·499	·508	·500	·511	·516	·530	·538	·550	·548
Nov	·476	·484	·475	·484	·489	·495	·501	·510	·502	·513	·518	·532	·540	·552	·550
Dec	·481	·489	·481	·489	·494	·501	·506	·515	·507	·519	·524	·537	·545	·557	·555
1993	May	June	July	Aug	Sep	Oct	Nov	Dec	Jan	Feb	Mar	Apr	May	June	July
Jan	·495	·503	·495	·503	·508	·515	·521	·529	·521	·533	·538	·552	·560	·572	·570
Feb	·486	·494	·485	·494	·499	·505	·511	·519	·512	·523	·528	·542	·550	·562	·560
Mar	·480	·488	·480	·488	·493	·500	·505	·514	·506	·518	·523	·536	·544	·556	·554
Apr	·467	·474	·466	·474	·479	·486	·491	·500	·492	·504	·509	·522	·530	·542	·540
May	·461	·469	·461	·469	·474	·481	·486	·495	·487	·498	·503	·517	·524	·536	·534
June	·462	·470	·462	·470	·475	·482	·487	·496	·488	·499	·504	·518	·526	·538	·635
July	·466	·473	·465	·473	·478	·485	·490	·499	·491	·502	·507	·521	·529	·541	·539
Aug	·459	·467	·459	·467	·472	·478	·484	·493	·485	·496	·501	·515	·522	·534	·532
Sept	·453	·461	·452	·461	·466	·472	·478	·486	·479	·490	·495	·508	·516	·528	·526
Oct	·454	·462	·453	·462	·467	·473	·479	·487	·480	·491	·496	·509	·517	·529	·527
Nov	·456	·464	·456	·464	·469	·475	·481	·489	·482	·493	·498	·511	·519	·531	·529
Dec	·453	·461	·452	·461	·466	·472	·478	·486	·479	·490	·495	·508	·516	·528	·526

MONTH OF DISPOSAL

	2006											2007			
1994	Feb	Mar	Apr	May	June	July	Aug	Sep	Oct	Nov	Dec	Jan	Feb	Mar	Apr
Jan	·374	·380	·391	·399	·405	·405	·410	·416	·418	·423	·435	·427	·437	·447	·454
Feb	·367	·372	·383	·391	·397	·397	·402	·408	·410	·415	·426	·419	·429	·438	·445
Mar	·363	·368	·379	·387	·393	·393	·398	·404	·406	·411	·422	·415	·425	·434	·441
Apr	·347	·352	·363	·371	·377	·377	·381	·388	·390	·395	·406	·398	·408	·417	·424
May	·342	·348	·358	·366	·372	·372	·377	·383	·385	·390	·401	·393	·404	·413	·419
June	·342	·348	·358	·366	·372	·372	·377	·383	·385	·390	·401	·393	·404	·413	·419
July	·349	·354	·365	·373	·378	·378	·383	·390	·392	·397	·408	·400	·410	·419	·426
Aug	·342	·348	·358	·366	·372	·372	·377	·383	·385	·390	·401	·393	·404	·413	·419
Sept	·339	·345	·355	·363	·369	·369	·374	·380	·382	·387	·398	·390	·401	·410	·417
Oct	·337	·343	·353	·362	·367	·367	·372	·378	·380	·385	·396	·388	·399	·408	·415
Nov	·337	·342	·352	·361	·366	·366	·371	·377	·379	·384	·395	·387	·398	·407	·414
Dec	·330	·336	·346	·354	·360	·360	·364	·371	·373	·377	·388	·381	·391	·400	·407
1995	Feb	Mar	Apr	May	June	July	Aug	Sep	Oct	Nov	Dec	Jan	Feb	Mar	Apr
Jan	·330	·336	·346	·354	·360	·360	·364	·371	·373	·377	·388	·381	·391	·400	·407
Feb	·322	·327	·338	·346	·351	·351	·356	·362	·364	·369	·380	·372	·383	·391	·398
Mar	·317	·322	·332	·340	·346	·346	·351	·357	·359	·363	·374	·367	·377	·386	·393
Apr	·303	·309	·319	·327	·332	·332	·337	·343	·345	·350	·360	·353	·363	·372	·379
May	·298	·303	·314	·322	·327	·327	·332	·338	·340	·344	·355	·348	·358	·366	·373
June	·296	·302	·312	·320	·325	·325	·330	·336	·338	·342	·353	·346	·356	·364	·371
July	·302	·308	·318	·326	·331	·331	·336	·342	·344	·349	·359	·352	·362	·371	·378
Aug	·296	·301	·311	·319	·324	·324	·329	·335	·337	·342	·352	·345	·355	·364	·370
Sept	·290	·295	·305	·313	·318	·318	·323	·329	·331	·335	·346	·339	·349	·357	·364
Oct	·296	·302	·312	·320	·325	·325	·330	·336	·338	·342	·353	·346	·356	·364	·371
Nov	·296	·302	·312	·320	·325	·325	·330	·336	·338	·342	·353	·346	·356	·364	·371
Dec	·289	·294	·304	·312	·317	·317	·322	·328	·330	·334	·345	·338	·348	·356	·363
1996	Feb	Mar	Apr	May	June	July	Aug	Sep	Oct	Nov	Dec	Jan	Feb	Mar	Apr
Jan	·293	·298	·308	·316	·322	·322	·326	·332	·334	·339	·350	·342	·352	·361	·368
Feb	·287	·292	·302	·310	·315	·315	·320	·326	·328	·333	·343	·336	·346	·355	·361
Mar	·282	·287	·297	·305	·310	·310	·315	·321	·323	·327	·338	·331	·341	·349	·356
Apr	·273	·278	·288	·296	·301	·301	·305	·311	·313	·318	·328	·321	·331	·339	·346
May	·270	·275	·285	·293	·298	·298	·303	·309	·311	·315	·326	·319	·328	·337	·343
June	·269	·275	·284	·292	·297	·297	·302	·308	·310	·314	·325	·318	·327	·336	·342
July	·274	·280	·289	·297	·302	·302	·307	·313	·315	·320	·330	·323	·333	·341	·348
Aug	·268	·274	·283	·291	·297	·297	·301	·307	·309	·314	·324	·317	·327	·335	·342
Sept	·263	·268	·278	·285	·291	·291	·295	·301	·303	·308	·318	·311	·321	·329	·336
Oct	·263	·268	·278	·285	·291	·291	·295	·301	·303	·308	·318	·311	·321	·329	·336
Nov	·262	·267	·277	·285	·290	·290	·294	·300	·302	·307	·317	·310	·320	·328	·335
Dec	·258	·263	·273	·280	·286	·286	·290	·296	·298	·302	·313	·306	·315	·324	·330
1997	Feb	Mar	Apr	May	June	July	Aug	Sep	Oct	Nov	Dec	Jan	Feb	Mar	Apr
Jan	·258	·263	·273	·280	·286	·286	·290	·296	·298	·302	·313	·306	·315	·324	·330
Feb	·253	·258	·268	·275	·281	·281	·285	·291	·293	·297	·308	·301	·310	·319	·325
Mar	·250	·255	·264	·272	·277	·277	·282	·288	·290	·294	·304	·297	·307	·315	·322
Apr	·242	·248	·257	·265	·270	·270	·274	·280	·282	·287	·297	·290	·299	·308	·314
May	·238	·243	·252	·260	·265	·265	·270	·275	·277	·282	·292	·285	·294	·303	·309
June	·233	·238	·248	·255	·260	·260	·265	·270	·272	·277	·287	·280	·290	·298	·304
July	·233	·238	·248	·255	·260	·260	·265	·270	·272	·277	·287	·280	·290	·298	·304
Aug	·225	·230	·240	·247	·252	·252	·257	·262	·264	·269	·279	·272	·281	·290	·296
Sept	·219	·224	·234	·241	·246	·246	·250	·256	·258	·262	·272	·266	·275	·283	·289
Oct	·218	·223	·232	·239	·245	·245	·249	·255	·256	·261	·271	·264	·273	·282	·288
Nov	·217	·222	·231	·239	·244	·244	·248	·254	·256	·260	·270	·263	·273	·281	·287
Dec	·214	·219	·228	·236	·241	·241	·245	·251	·253	·257	·267	·260	·269	·278	·284

MONTH OF DISPOSAL

	2007								2008						
1994	May	June	July	Aug	Sep	Oct	Nov	Dec	Jan	Feb	Mar	Apr	May	June	July
Jan	·459	·467	·459	·467	·472	·478	·484	·493	·485	·496	·501	·515	·522	·534	·532
Feb	·451	·459	·450	·459	·464	·470	·476	·484	·476	·488	·493	·506	·514	·526	·524
Mar	·447	·455	·446	·455	·460	·466	·472	·480	·472	·484	·488	·502	·509	·521	·519
Apr	·430	·438	·429	·438	·442	·449	·454	·463	·455	·466	·471	·484	·492	·503	·501
May	·425	·433	·424	·433	·437	·444	·449	·457	·450	·461	·466	·479	·487	·498	·496
June	·425	·433	·424	·433	·437	·444	·449	·457	·450	·461	·466	·479	·487	·498	·496
July	·432	·440	·431	·440	·444	·451	·456	·465	·457	·468	·473	·486	·494	·506	·503
Aug	·425	·433	·424	·433	·437	·444	·449	·457	·450	·461	·466	·479	·487	·498	·496
Sept	·422	·430	·421	·430	·434	·441	·446	·454	·447	·458	·463	·476	·483	·495	·493
Oct	·420	·428	·419	·428	·433	·439	·444	·452	·445	·456	·461	·474	·481	·493	·491
Nov	·419	·427	·418	·427	·432	·438	·443	·451	·444	·455	·460	·473	·480	·492	·490
Dec	·412	·420	·412	·420	·425	·431	·436	·445	·437	·448	·453	·466	·473	·485	·483
1995	May	June	July	Aug	Sep	Oct	Nov	Dec	Jan	Feb	Mar	Apr	May	June	July
Jan	·412	·420	·412	·420	·425	·431	·436	·445	·437	·448	·453	·466	·473	·485	·483
Feb	·404	·411	·403	·411	·416	·422	·428	·436	·428	·439	·444	·457	·464	·476	·474
Mar	·398	·405	·397	·405	·410	·416	·422	·430	·422	·433	·438	·451	·458	·470	·468
Apr	·384	·391	·383	·391	·396	·402	·407	·415	·408	·419	·423	·436	·444	·455	·453
May	·378	·386	·378	·386	·390	·396	·402	·410	·402	·413	·418	·430	·438	·449	·447
June	·377	·384	·376	·384	·389	·395	·400	·408	·401	·411	·416	·429	·436	·447	·445
July	·383	·390	·382	·390	·395	·401	·406	·414	·407	·418	·423	·435	·443	·454	·452
Aug	·376	·383	·375	·383	·388	·394	·399	·407	·400	·410	·415	·428	·435	·446	·444
Sept	·369	·376	·369	·376	·381	·387	·392	·400	·393	·404	·408	·421	·428	·440	·438
Oct	·377	·384	·376	·384	·389	·395	·400	·408	·401	·411	·416	·429	·436	·447	·445
Nov	·377	·384	·376	·384	·389	·395	·400	·408	·401	·411	·416	·429	·436	·447	·445
Dec	·368	·376	·368	·376	·380	·386	·392	·399	·392	·403	·407	·420	·427	·439	·437
1996	May	June	July	Aug	Sep	Oct	Nov	Dec	Jan	Feb	Mar	Apr	May	June	July
Jan	·373	·380	·372	·380	·385	·391	·396	·404	·397	·407	·412	·425	·432	·443	·441
Feb	·366	·374	·366	·374	·378	·384	·390	·398	·390	·401	·406	·418	·425	·437	·435
Mar	·361	·368	·360	·368	·373	·379	·384	·392	·385	·395	·400	·413	·420	·431	·429
Apr	·351	·358	·351	·358	·363	·369	·374	·382	·375	·385	·390	·402	·410	·421	·419
May	·349	·356	·348	·356	·360	·366	·371	·379	·372	·383	·387	·400	·407	·418	·416
June	·348	·355	·347	·355	·359	·365	·371	·378	·371	·382	·386	·399	·406	·417	·415
July	·353	·360	·352	·360	·365	·371	·376	·384	·377	·387	·392	·404	·411	·423	·421
Aug	·347	·354	·346	·354	·359	·364	·370	·378	·370	·381	·385	·398	·405	·416	·414
Sept	·341	·348	·340	·348	·352	·358	·363	·371	·364	·375	·379	·391	·399	·410	·408
Oct	·341	·348	·340	·348	·352	·358	·363	·371	·364	·375	·379	·391	·399	·410	·408
Nov	·340	·347	·339	·347	·352	·357	·363	·370	·363	·374	·378	·391	·398	·409	·407
Dec	·335	·343	·335	·343	·347	·353	·358	·366	·359	·369	·374	·386	·393	·404	·402
1997	May	June	July	Aug	Sep	Oct	Nov	Dec	Jan	Feb	Mar	Apr	May	June	July
Jan	·335	·343	·335	·343	·347	·353	·358	·366	·359	·369	·374	·386	·393	·404	·402
Feb	·330	·337	·330	·337	·342	·348	·353	·361	·354	·364	·368	·381	·388	·399	·397
Mar	·327	·334	·326	·334	·338	·344	·349	·357	·350	·360	·365	·377	·384	·395	·393
Apr	·319	·326	·319	·326	·331	·337	·342	·349	·342	·353	·357	·369	·376	·387	·385
May	·314	·321	·314	·321	·326	·331	·337	·344	·337	·347	·352	·364	·371	·382	·380
June	·309	·316	·309	·316	·321	·326	·331	·339	·332	·342	·347	·359	·366	·377	·375
July	·309	·316	·309	·316	·321	·326	·331	·339	·332	·342	·347	·359	·366	·377	·375
Aug	·301	·308	·300	·308	·312	·318	·323	·331	·324	·334	·338	·350	·357	·368	·366
Sept	·294	·301	·294	·301	·306	·311	·316	·324	·317	·327	·331	·343	·350	·361	·359
Oct	·293	·300	·292	·300	·304	·310	·315	·322	·315	·325	·330	·342	·349	·359	·357
Nov	·292	·299	·291	·299	·303	·309	·314	·321	·315	·325	·329	·341	·348	·358	·357
Dec	·289	·296	·288	·296	·300	·306	·311	·318	·311	·321	·326	·338	·344	·355	·353

MONTH OF DISPOSAL

	2006											2007			
1998	Feb	Mar	Apr	May	June	July	Aug	Sep	Oct	Nov	Dec	Jan	Feb	Mar	Apr
Jan	·218	·223	·232	·239	·245	·245	·249	·255	·256	·261	·271	·264	·273	·282	·288
Feb	·211	·216	·226	·233	·238	·238	·243	·248	·250	·255	·265	·258	·267	·275	·281
Mar	·208	·213	·222	·229	·234	·234	·239	·244	·246	·251	·261	·254	·263	·271	·277
Apr	·194	·199	·208	·216	·221	·221	·225	·231	·232	·237	·247	·240	·249	·257	·263
May	·188	·193	·202	·209	·214	·214	·218	·224	·226	·230	·240	·233	·242	·250	·256
June	·188	·193	·203	·210	·215	·215	·219	·225	·226	·231	·241	·234	·243	·251	·257
July	·191	·196	·206	·213	·218	·218	·222	·228	·229	·234	·244	·237	·246	·254	·260
Aug	·186	·191	·200	·208	·213	·213	·217	·222	·224	·228	·238	·232	·241	·249	·255
Sept	·181	·186	·195	·203	·207	·207	·212	·217	·219	·223	·233	·226	·235	·243	·249
Oct	·181	·185	·195	·202	·207	·207	·211	·216	·218	·222	·232	·226	·235	·243	·249
Nov	·181	·186	·195	·203	·207	·207	·212	·217	·219	·223	·233	·226	·235	·243	·249
Dec	·181	·186	·195	·203	·207	·207	·212	·217	·219	·223	·233	·226	·235	·243	·249
1999	Feb	Mar	Apr	May	June	July	Aug	Sep	Oct	Nov	Dec	Jan	Feb	Mar	Apr
Jan	·188	·193	·203	·210	·215	·215	·219	·225	·226	·231	·241	·234	·243	·251	·257
Feb	·186	·191	·200	·208	·213	·213	·217	·222	·224	·228	·238	·232	·241	·249	·255
Mar	·183	·188	·197	·205	·210	·210	·214	·219	·221	·225	·235	·229	·238	·246	·252
Apr	·176	·180	·189	·197	·202	·202	·206	·211	·213	·217	·227	·220	·229	·237	·243
May	·173	·178	·187	·194	·199	·199	·203	·208	·210	·214	·224	·217	·226	·234	·240
June	·173	·178	·187	·194	·199	·199	·203	·208	·210	·214	·224	·217	·226	·234	·240
July	·176	·181	·190	·197	·202	·202	·207	·212	·214	·218	·228	·221	·230	·238	·244
Aug	·173	·178	·187	·195	·199	·199	·204	·209	·211	·215	·225	·218	·227	·235	·241
Sept	·168	·173	·182	·190	·194	·194	·199	·204	·206	·210	·220	·213	·222	·230	·236
Oct	·166	·171	·180	·187	·192	·192	·196	·202	·204	·208	·217	·211	·220	·228	·234
Nov	·165	·170	·179	·186	·191	·191	·195	·200	·202	·206	·216	·209	·218	·226	·232
Dec	·161	·166	·175	·182	·186	·186	·191	·196	·198	·202	·212	·205	·214	·222	·228
2000	Feb	Mar	Apr	May	June	July	Aug	Sep	Oct	Nov	Dec	Jan	Feb	Mar	Apr
Jan	·166	·170	·179	·187	·191	·191	·196	·201	·203	·207	·217	·210	·219	·227	·233
Feb	·159	·164	·173	·180	·185	·185	·189	·195	·196	·201	·210	·204	·213	·220	·226
Mar	·153	·158	·167	·174	·179	·179	·183	·188	·190	·194	·204	·197	·206	·214	·220
Apr	·142	·146	·155	·162	·167	·167	·171	·176	·178	·182	·192	·185	·194	·202	·208
May	·138	·142	·151	·158	·163	·163	·167	·172	·174	·178	·187	·181	·190	·197	·203
June	·135	·140	·148	·155	·160	·160	·164	·169	·171	·175	·185	·178	·187	·195	·200
July	·139	·144	·152	·160	·164	·164	·168	·174	·175	·179	·189	·182	·191	·199	·205
Aug	·139	·144	·152	·160	·164	·164	·168	·174	·175	·179	·189	·182	·191	·199	·205
Sept	·131	·136	·144	·151	·156	·156	·160	·165	·167	·171	·181	·174	·183	·190	·196
Oct	·132	·136	·145	·152	·157	·157	·161	·166	·168	·172	·181	·175	·184	·191	·197
Nov	·128	·133	·142	·149	·153	·153	·157	·163	·164	·169	·178	·171	·180	·188	·193
Dec	·128	·132	·141	·148	·153	·153	·157	·162	·164	·168	·177	·171	·179	·187	·193
2001	Feb	Mar	Apr	May	June	July	Aug	Sep	Oct	Nov	Dec	Jan	Feb	Mar	Apr
Jan	·135	·140	·148	·155	·160	·160	·164	·169	·171	·175	·185	·178	·187	·195	·200
Feb	·129	·134	·142	·149	·154	·154	·158	·163	·165	·169	·178	·172	·181	·188	·194
Mar	·128	·132	·141	·148	·153	·153	·157	·162	·164	·168	·177	·171	·179	·187	·193
Apr	·122	·127	·135	·142	·147	·147	·151	·156	·158	·162	·171	·165	·173	·181	·187
May	·115	·119	·128	·135	·139	·139	·144	·149	·150	·154	·164	·157	·166	·173	·179
June	·114	·118	·127	·134	·138	·138	·142	·147	·149	·153	·162	·156	·165	·172	·178
July	·121	·125	·134	·141	·145	·145	·149	·155	·156	·160	·170	·163	·172	·179	·185
Aug	·116	·121	·129	·136	·141	·141	·145	·150	·152	·156	·165	·159	·167	·175	·180
Sept	·112	·117	·125	·132	·137	·137	·141	·146	·148	·152	·161	·155	·163	·171	·176
Oct	·114	·119	·127	·134	·139	·139	·143	·148	·150	·154	·163	·157	·165	·173	·178
Nov	·119	·123	·132	·139	·143	·143	·147	·153	·154	·158	·168	·161	·170	·177	·183
Dec	·120	·125	·133	·140	·145	·145	·149	·154	·156	·160	·169	·163	·171	·179	·185

MONTH OF DISPOSAL

	2007								2008						
1998	May	June	July	Aug	Sep	Oct	Nov	Dec	Jan	Feb	Mar	Apr	May	June	July
Jan	·293	·300	·292	·300	·304	·310	·315	·322	·315	·325	·330	·342	·349	·359	·357
Feb	·286	·293	·286	·293	·298	·303	·308	·316	·309	·319	·323	·335	·342	·352	·351
Mar	·282	·289	·282	·289	·294	·299	·304	·312	·305	·315	·319	·331	·338	·348	·346
Apr	·268	·275	·268	·275	·279	·285	·290	·297	·290	·300	·304	·316	·323	·333	·331
May	·261	·268	·261	·268	·272	·278	·283	·290	·283	·293	·297	·309	·316	·326	·324
June	·262	·269	·261	·269	·273	·278	·283	·291	·284	·294	·298	·310	·316	·327	·325
July	·265	·272	·264	·272	·276	·282	·287	·294	·287	·297	·301	·313	·320	·330	·328
Aug	·260	·266	·259	·266	·271	·276	·281	·288	·282	·291	·296	·307	·314	·324	·323
Sept	·254	·261	·254	·261	·265	·271	·276	·283	·276	·286	·290	·302	·308	·319	·317
Oct	·253	·260	·253	·260	·264	·270	·275	·282	·275	·285	·289	·301	·308	·318	·316
Nov	·254	·261	·254	·261	·265	·271	·276	·283	·276	·286	·290	·302	·308	·319	·317
Dec	·254	·261	·254	·261	·265	·271	·276	·283	·276	·286	·290	·302	·308	·319	·317
1999	May	June	July	Aug	Sep	Oct	Nov	Dec	Jan	Feb	Mar	Apr	May	June	July
Jan	·262	·269	·261	·269	·273	·278	·283	·291	·284	·294	·298	·310	·316	·327	·325
Feb	·260	·266	·259	·266	·271	·276	·281	·288	·282	·291	·296	·307	·314	·324	·323
Mar	·257	·263	·256	·263	·268	·273	·278	·285	·278	·288	·293	·304	·311	·321	·319
Apr	·248	·255	·248	·255	·259	·265	·269	·277	·270	·280	·284	·295	·302	·312	·311
May	·245	·252	·245	·252	·256	·261	·266	·274	·267	·277	·281	·292	·299	·309	·307
June	·245	·252	·245	·252	·256	·261	·266	·274	·267	·277	·281	·292	·299	·309	·307
July	·249	·256	·248	·256	·260	·265	·270	·277	·271	·280	·285	·296	·303	·313	·311
Aug	·246	·253	·245	·253	·257	·262	·267	·274	·268	·277	·282	·293	·300	·310	·308
Sept	·241	·247	·240	·247	·252	·257	·262	·269	·262	·272	·276	·288	·294	·304	·303
Oct	·238	·245	·238	·245	·249	·255	·259	·267	·260	·270	·274	·285	·292	·302	·300
Nov	·237	·244	·236	·244	·248	·253	·258	·265	·259	·268	·272	·284	·290	·301	·299
Dec	·233	·239	·232	·239	·243	·249	·253	·261	·254	·264	·268	·279	·286	·296	·294
2000	May	June	July	Aug	Sep	Oct	Nov	Dec	Jan	Feb	Mar	Apr	May	June	July
Jan	·238	·244	·237	·244	·248	·254	·259	·266	·259	·269	·273	·285	·291	·301	·300
Feb	·231	·238	·230	·238	·242	·247	·252	·259	·253	·262	·266	·278	·284	·294	·293
Mar	·224	·231	·224	·231	·235	·240	·245	·252	·246	·255	·260	·271	·277	·287	·286
Apr	·212	·219	·212	·219	·223	·228	·233	·240	·233	·243	·247	·258	·265	·275	·273
May	·208	·214	·207	·214	·219	·224	·228	·236	·229	·238	·243	·254	·260	·270	·268
June	·205	·212	·205	·212	·216	·221	·226	·233	·226	·236	·240	·251	·257	·267	·265
July	·209	·216	·209	·216	·220	·225	·230	·237	·230	·240	·244	·255	·262	·272	·270
Aug	·209	·216	·209	·216	·220	·225	·230	·237	·230	·240	·244	·255	·262	·272	·207
Sept	·201	·207	·200	·207	·211	·217	·221	·228	·222	·231	·235	·246	·253	·263	·261
Oct	·202	·208	·201	·208	·212	·217	·222	·229	·223	·232	·236	·247	·253	·263	·262
Nov	·198	·205	·198	·205	·209	·214	·218	·225	·219	·228	·232	·243	·250	·260	·258
Dec	·197	·204	·197	·204	·208	·213	·218	·225	·218	·228	·232	·243	·249	·259	·257
2001	May	June	July	Aug	Sep	Oct	Nov	Dec	Jan	Feb	Mar	Apr	May	June	July
Jan	·205	·212	·205	·212	·216	·221	·226	·233	·226	·236	·240	·251	·257	·267	·265
Feb	·199	·205	·198	·205	·209	·215	·219	·226	·220	·229	·233	·244	·251	·260	·259
Mar	·197	·204	·197	·204	·208	·213	·218	·225	·218	·228	·232	·243	·249	·259	·257
Apr	·191	·198	·191	·198	·202	·207	·211	·218	·212	·221	·225	·236	·243	·252	·251
May	·184	·190	·183	·190	·194	·199	·204	·211	·204	·214	·218	·228	·235	·245	·243
June	·182	·189	·182	·189	·193	·198	·202	·209	·203	·212	·216	·227	·233	·243	·241
July	·190	·196	·189	·196	·200	·205	·210	·217	·211	·220	·224	·235	·241	·251	·249
Aug	·185	·191	·184	·191	·195	·201	·205	·212	·206	·215	·219	·230	·236	·246	·244
Sept	·181	·187	·180	·187	·191	·196	·201	·208	·202	·211	·215	·226	·232	·242	·240
Oct	·183	·189	·182	·189	·193	·199	·203	·290	·204	·213	·217	·228	·234	·244	·242
Nov	·188	·194	·187	·194	·198	·203	·208	·215	·209	·218	·222	·233	·239	·249	·247
Dec	·189	·196	·189	·196	·200	·205	·209	·216	·210	·219	·223	·234	·240	·250	·249

MONTH OF DISPOSAL

	2006											2007			
2002	Feb	Mar	Apr	May	June	July	Aug	Sep	Oct	Nov	Dec	Jan	Feb	Mar	Apr
Jan	·121	·125	·134	·141	·145	·145	·149	·155	·156	·160	·170	·163	·172	·179	·185
Feb	·117	·122	·131	·138	·142	·142	·146	·151	·153	·157	·166	·160	·169	·176	·182
Mar	·113	·117	·126	·133	·138	·138	·142	·147	·148	·152	·162	·155	·164	·171	·177
Apr	·105	·110	·118	·125	·130	·130	·134	·139	·141	·145	·154	·147	·156	·163	·169
May	·102	·107	·115	·122	·127	·127	·131	·136	·137	·141	·150	·144	·153	·160	·166
June	·102	·107	·115	·122	·127	·127	·131	·136	·137	·141	·150	·144	·153	·160	·166
July	·104	·109	·117	·124	·128	·128	·132	·138	·139	·143	·152	·146	·155	·162	·168
Aug	·101	·105	·114	·121	·125	·125	·129	·134	·136	·140	·149	·143	·151	·159	·164
Sept	·093	·098	·106	·113	·118	·118	·122	·127	·128	·132	·141	·135	·144	·151	·157
Oct	·092	·096	·105	·111	·116	·116	·120	·125	·126	·130	·139	·133	·142	·149	·155
Nov	·090	·094	·103	·109	·114	·114	·118	·123	·125	·129	·137	·131	·140	·147	·153
Dec	·088	·092	·101	·108	·112	·112	·116	·121	·123	·127	·136	·129	·138	·145	·151
2003	Feb	Mar	Apr	May	June	July	Aug	Sep	Oct	Nov	Dec	Jan	Feb	Mar	Apr
Jan	·089	·093	·101	·108	·113	·113	·117	·122	·123	·127	·136	·130	·138	·146	·151
Feb	·083	·088	·096	·103	·107	·107	·111	·116	·118	·122	·131	·124	·133	·140	·146
Mar	·079	·084	·092	·099	·103	·103	·107	·112	·114	·118	·127	·121	·129	·136	·142
Apr	·072	·076	·084	·091	·095	·095	·099	·104	·106	·110	·119	·113	·121	·128	·134
May	·070	·074	·083	·089	·094	·094	·098	·102	·104	·108	·117	·111	·119	·126	·132
June	·071	·076	·084	·090	·095	·095	·099	·104	·105	·109	·118	·112	·120	·127	·133
July	·071	·076	·084	·090	·095	·095	·099	·104	·105	·109	·118	·112	·120	·127	·133
Aug	·069	·074	·082	·089	·093	·093	·097	·102	·104	·107	·116	·110	·118	·126	·131
Sept	·064	·068	·077	·083	·088	·088	·092	·096	·098	·102	·111	·105	·113	·120	·125
Oct	·064	·068	·076	·083	·087	·087	·091	·096	·097	·101	·110	·104	·112	·119	·125
Nov	·063	·067	·076	·082	·086	·086	·090	·095	·097	·101	·109	·103	·112	·119	·124
Dec	·058	·063	·071	·077	·082	·082	·086	·090	·092	·096	·105	·099	·107	·114	·119
2004	Feb	Mar	Apr	May	June	July	Aug	Sep	Oct	Nov	Dec	Jan	Feb	Mar	Apr
Jan	·061	·065	·073	·080	·084	·084	·088	·093	·094	·098	·107	·101	·109	·116	·122
Feb	·057	·061	·069	·076	·080	·080	·084	·089	·090	·094	·103	·097	·105	·112	·118
Mar	·052	·056	·064	·071	·075	·075	·079	·084	·086	·089	·098	·092	·100	·107	·113
Apr	·046	·050	·058	·065	·069	·069	·073	·078	·079	·083	·092	·086	·094	·101	·106
May	·041	·046	·054	·060	·064	·064	·068	·073	·075	·078	·087	·081	·089	·096	·101
June	·040	·044	·052	·058	·063	·063	·066	·071	·073	·077	·085	·079	·087	·094	·100
July	·040	·044	·052	·058	·063	·063	·066	·071	·073	·077	·085	·079	·087	·094	·100
Aug	·036	·041	·049	·055	·059	·059	·063	·068	·069	·073	·082	·076	·084	·091	·096
Sept	·032	·037	·045	·051	·055	·055	·059	·064	·065	·069	·078	·072	·080	·087	·092
Oct	·030	·034	·042	·048	·052	·052	·056	·061	·063	·066	·075	·069	·077	·084	·089
Nov	·028	·032	·040	·046	·050	·050	·054	·059	·060	·064	·072	·067	·075	·081	·087
Dec	·023	·027	·035	·041	·045	·045	·049	·054	·055	·059	·067	·062	·070	·076	·082
2005	Feb	Mar	Apr	May	June	July	Aug	Sep	Oct	Nov	Dec	Jan	Feb	Mar	Apr
Jan	·028	·032	·040	·047	·051	·051	·055	·059	·061	·065	·073	·067	·075	·082	·087
Feb	·024	·028	·036	·043	·047	·047	·051	·055	·057	·061	·069	·063	·071	·078	·083
Mar	·019	·024	·031	·038	·042	·042	·046	·050	·052	·056	·064	·058	·066	·073	·078
Apr	·014	·018	·026	·032	·036	·036	·040	·044	·046	·050	·058	·052	·060	·067	·072
May	·011	·016	·023	·030	·034	·034	·037	·042	·044	·047	·056	·050	·058	·065	·070
June	·010	·015	·022	·029	·033	·033	·036	·041	·043	·046	·055	·049	·057	·063	·069
July	·010	·015	·022	·029	·033	·033	·036	·041	·043	·046	·055	·049	·057	·063	·069
Aug	·008	·012	·020	·026	·031	·031	·034	·039	·040	·044	·052	·047	·055	·061	·066
Sept	·006	·010	·018	·024	·028	·028	·032	·036	·038	·041	·050	·044	·052	·059	·064
Oct	·005	·009	·017	·023	·027	·027	·031	·035	·037	·040	·049	·043	·051	·057	·063
Nov	·003	·007	·015	·021	·025	·025	·029	·034	·035	·039	·047	·041	·049	·056	·061
Dec	·001	·005	·012	·019	·023	·023	·026	·031	·032	·036	·044	·039	·046	·053	·058

MONTH OF DISPOSAL

	2007								2008						
2002	May	June	July	Aug	Sep	Oct	Nov	Dec	Jan	Feb	Mar	Apr	May	June	July
Jan	·190	·196	·189	·196	·200	·205	·210	·217	·211	·220	·224	·235	·241	·251	·249
Feb	·186	·193	·186	·193	·197	·202	·207	·213	·207	·216	·220	·231	·238	·247	·246
Mar	·182	·188	·181	·188	·192	·197	·202	·209	·202	·211	·215	·226	·233	·242	·241
Apr	·174	·180	·173	·180	·184	·189	·194	·200	·194	·203	·207	·218	·224	·234	·232
May	·170	·177	·170	·177	·180	·186	·190	·197	·191	·200	·204	·215	·221	·230	·229
June	·170	·177	·170	·177	·180	·186	·190	·197	·191	·200	·204	·215	·221	·230	·229
July	·172	·179	·172	·179	·182	·188	·192	·199	·193	·202	·206	·217	·223	·233	·231
Aug	·169	·175	·168	·175	·179	·184	·189	·196	·189	·198	·202	·213	·219	·229	·227
Sept	·161	·167	·160	·167	·171	·176	·181	·188	·181	·190	·194	·205	·211	·221	·219
Oct	·159	·165	·159	·165	·169	·174	·179	·185	·179	·188	·192	·203	·209	·219	·217
Nov	·157	·163	·157	·163	·167	·172	·177	·184	·177	·186	·190	·201	·207	·217	·215
Dec	·155	·161	·155	·161	·165	·170	·175	·182	·175	·184	·188	·199	·205	·215	·213
2003	May	June	July	Aug	Sep	Oct	Nov	Dec	Jan	Feb	Mar	Apr	May	June	July
Jan	·156	·162	·155	·162	·166	·171	·175	·182	·176	·185	·189	·200	·206	·215	·214
Feb	·150	·156	·149	·156	·160	·165	·170	·176	·170	·179	·183	·194	·200	·209	·207
Mar	·146	·152	·146	·152	·156	·161	·166	·172	·166	·175	·179	·190	·196	·205	·203
Apr	·138	·144	·137	·144	·148	·153	·157	·164	·158	·167	·171	·181	·187	·196	·195
May	·136	·142	·136	·142	·146	·151	·155	·162	·156	·165	·169	·179	·185	·194	·193
June	·137	·143	·137	·143	·147	·152	·157	·163	·157	·166	·170	·180	·186	·196	·194
July	·137	·143	·137	·143	·147	·152	·157	·163	·157	·166	·170	·180	·186	·196	·194
Aug	·135	·142	·135	·142	·145	·150	·155	·161	·155	·164	·168	·178	·184	·194	·192
Sept	·130	·136	·129	·136	·140	·145	·149	·156	·150	·158	·162	·173	·179	·188	·186
Oct	·129	·135	·129	·135	·139	·144	·148	·155	·149	·158	·162	·172	·178	·187	·186
Nov	·129	·135	·128	·135	·138	·1438	·148	·154	·148	·157	·161	·171	·177	·187	·185
Dec	·124	·130	·123	·130	·134	·138	·143	·149	·143	·152	·156	·166	·172	·181	·180
2004	May	June	July	Aug	Sep	Oct	Nov	Dec	Jan	Feb	Mar	Apr	May	June	July
Jan	·126	·132	·126	·132	·136	·141	·145	·152	·146	·155	·158	·169	·175	·184	·182
Feb	·122	·128	·121	·128	·132	·137	·141	·147	·141	·150	·154	·164	·170	·180	·178
Mar	·117	·123	·116	·123	·127	·132	·136	·142	·137	·145	·149	·159	·165	·174	·173
Apr	·110	·116	·110	·116	·120	·125	·129	·136	·130	·138	·142	·152	·158	·167	·166
May	·106	·112	·105	·112	·115	·120	·124	·131	·125	·134	·137	·147	·153	·162	·161
June	·104	·110	·103	·110	·113	·118	·123	·129	·123	·132	·135	·146	·151	·161	·159
July	·104	·110	·103	·110	·113	·118	·123	·129	·123	·132	·135	·146	·151	·161	·159
Aug	·100	·106	·100	·106	·110	·115	·119	·125	·120	·123	·132	·142	·148	·157	·155
Sept	·096	·102	·096	·102	·106	·111	·115	·121	·115	·124	·128	·138	·144	·153	·151
Oct	·093	·099	·093	·099	·103	·108	·112	·118	·112	·121	·125	·135	·141	·150	·148
Nov	·091	·097	·090	·097	·101	·105	·110	·116	·110	·119	·122	·132	·138	·147	·146
Dec	·086	·092	·085	·092	·095	·100	·104	·111	·105	·113	·117	·127	·133	·142	·140
2005	May	June	July	Aug	Sep	Oct	Nov	Dec	Jan	Feb	Mar	Apr	May	June	July
Jan	·092	·097	·091	·097	·101	·106	·110	·116	·111	·119	·123	·133	·139	·148	·146
Feb	·088	·093	·087	·093	·097	·102	·106	·112	·107	·115	·119	·129	·134	·143	·142
Mar	·082	·088	·082	·088	·092	·097	·101	·107	·101	·110	·113	·123	·129	·138	·136
Apr	·076	·082	·076	·082	·086	·090	·094	·101	·095	·103	·107	·117	·123	·132	·130
May	·074	·080	·073	·080	·083	·088	·092	·098	·093	·101	·105	·115	·120	·129	·128
June	·073	·079	·072	·079	·082	·087	·091	·097	·092	·100	·104	·113	·119	·128	·126
July	·073	·079	·072	·079	·082	·087	·091	·097	·092	·100	·104	·113	·119	·128	·126
Aug	·071	·076	·070	·076	·080	·085	·089	·095	·089	·098	·101	·111	·117	·126	·124
Sept	·068	·074	·067	·074	·077	·082	·086	·092	·086	·095	·098	·108	·114	·123	·121
Oct	·067	·072	·066	·072	·076	·081	·085	·091	·085	·094	·097	·107	·113	·122	·120
Nov	·065	·071	·065	·071	·074	·079	·083	·089	·084	·092	·096	·105	·111	·120	·118
Dec	·062	·068	·062	·068	·072	·076	·080	·087	·081	·089	·093	·103	·108	·117	·115

MONTH OF DISPOSAL

2006	2006											2007			
2006	Feb	Mar	Apr	May	June	July	Aug	Sep	Oct	Nov	Dec	Jan	Feb	Mar	Apr
Jan	·004	·008	·016	·022	·026	·026	·030	·035	·036	·040	·048	·042	·050	·057	·062
Feb	·000	·004	·012	·018	·022	·022	·026	·030	·032	·036	·044	·038	·046	·053	·058
Mar	—	·000	·008	·014	·018	·018	·022	·026	·028	·031	·039	·034	·042	·048	·053
Apr	—	—	·000	·014	·010	·010	·014	·018	·020	·023	·032	·026	·034	·040	·045
May	—	—	—	·000	·004	·004	·008	·012	·014	·017	·025	·020	·027	·034	·039
June	—	—	—	—	·000	·000	·004	·008	·010	·013	·021	·016	·023	·030	·035
July	—	—	—	—	—	·000	·004	·008	·010	·013	·021	·016	·023	·030	·035
Aug	—	—	—	—	—	—	·000	·005	·006	·010	·018	·012	·020	·026	·031
Sept	—	—	—	—	—	—	—	·000	·001	·005	·013	·007	·015	·021	·026
Oct	—	—	—	—	—	—	—	—	·000	·003	·011	·006	·013	·020	·025
Nov	—	—	—	—	—	—	—	—	—	·000	·008	·002	·010	·016	·021
Dec	—	—	—	—	—	—	—	—	—	—	·000	·000	·002	·008	·013
2007	Feb	Mar	Apr	May	June	July	Aug	Sep	Oct	Nov	Dec	Jan	Feb	Mar	Apr
Jan	—	—	—	—	—	—	—	—	—	—	—	·000	·007	·014	·019
Feb	—	—	—	—	—	—	—	—	—	—	—	—	·000	·006	·011
Mar	—	—	—	—	—	—	—	—	—	—	—	—	—	·000	·005
Apr	—	—	—	—	—	—	—	—	—	—	—	—	—	—	·005
May	—	—	—	—	—	—	—	—	—	—	—	—	—	—	—
June	—	—	—	—	—	—	—	—	—	—	—	—	—	—	—
July	—	—	—	—	—	—	—	—	—	—	—	—	—	—	—
Aug	—	—	—	—	—	—	—	—	—	—	—	—	—	—	—
Sep	—	—	—	—	—	—	—	—	—	—	—	—	—	—	—
Oct	—	—	—	—	—	—	—	—	—	—	—	—	—	—	—
Nov	—	—	—	—	—	—	—	—	—	—	—	—	—	—	—
Dec	—	—	—	—	—	—	—	—	—	—	—	—	—	—	—
2008	Feb	Mar	Apr	May	June	July	Aug	Sep	Oct	Nov	Dec	Jan	Feb	Mar	Apr
Jan	—	—	—	—	—	—	—	—	—	—	—	—	—	—	—
Feb	—	—	—	—	—	—	—	—	—	—	—	—	—	—	—
Mar	—	—	—	—	—	—	—	—	—	—	—	—	—	—	—
Apr	—	—	—	—	—	—	—	—	—	—	—	—	—	—	—
May	—	—	—	—	—	—	—	—	—	—	—	—	—	—	—
June	—	—	—	—	—	—	—	—	—	—	—	—	—	—	—
July	—	—	—	—	—	—	—	—	—	—	—	—	—	—	—

MONTH OF DISPOSAL

2007	2007								2008						
2006	May	June	July	Aug	Sep	Oct	Nov	Dec	Jan	Feb	Mar	Apr	May	June	July
Jan	·066	·072	·066	·072	·075	·080	·084	·090	·085	·093	·097	·107	·112	·121	·119
Feb	·062	·067	·061	·067	·071	·076	·080	·086	·080	·089	·092	·102	·108	·116	·115
Mar	·057	·063	·057	·063	·067	·071	·075	·082	·076	·084	·088	·097	·103	·112	·110
Apr	·049	·055	·049	·055	·059	·063	·067	·073	·068	·076	·079	·089	·095	·103	·102
May	·043	·049	·042	·049	·052	·057	·061	·067	·061	·069	·073	·082	·088	·097	·095
June	·039	·044	·038	·044	·048	·052	·056	·062	·057	·065	·069	·078	·084	·092	·091
July	·039	·044	·038	·044	·048	·052	·056	·062	·057	·065	·069	·078	·084	·092	·091
Aug	·035	·041	·035	·041	·044	·049	·053	·059	·053	·061	·065	·074	·080	·088	·087
Sept	·030	·036	·030	·036	·039	·044	·048	·054	·048	·056	·060	·069	·075	·083	·082
Oct	·029	·034	·028	·034	·038	·042	·046	·052	·047	·055	·058	·068	·073	·082	·080
Nov	·025	·031	·025	·031	·034	·039	·043	·049	·043	·051	·055	·064	·070	·078	·077
Dec	·017	·023	·017	·023	·026	·031	·035	·040	·035	·043	·046	·056	·061	·070	·068
2007	May	June	July	Aug	Sep	Oct	Nov	Dec	Jan	Feb	Mar	Apr	May	June	July
Jan	·023	·028	·022	·028	·032	·036	·040	·046	·041	·049	·052	·062	·067	·075	·074
Feb	·015	·021	·015	·021	·024	·029	·032	·038	·033	·041	·044	·054	·059	·067	·066
Mar	·009	·014	·008	·014	·018	·022	·026	·032	·026	·034	·038	·047	·052	·061	·059
Apr	·004	·009	·003	·009	·013	·017	·021	·027	·021	·029	·033	·042	·047	·056	·054
May	·000	·005	·000	·005	·009	·013	·017	·023	·017	·025	·029	·038	·043	·051	·050
June	—	·000	·000	·000	·003	·008	·012	·017	·012	·020	·023	·032	·038	·046	·044
July	—	—	·000	·006	·009	·014	·017	·023	·018	·026	·029	·038	·044	·052	·050
Aug	—	—	—	·000	·003	·008	·012	·017	·012	·020	·023	·032	·038	·046	·044
Sep	—	—	—	—	·000	·004	·008	·014	·009	·016	·020	·029	·034	·042	·041
Oct	—	—	—	—	—	·000	·004	·010	·004	·012	·015	·024	·030	·038	·036
Nov	—	—	—	—	—	—	·000	·006	·000	·008	·011	·021	·026	·034	·032
Dec	—	—	—	—	—	—	—	·000	·000	·002	·006	·015	·020	·028	·027
2008	May	Jun	Jul	Aug	Sep	Oct	Nov	Dec	Jan	Feb	Mar	Apr	May	June	July
Jan	—	—	—	—	—	—	—	—	·000	·008	·011	·020	·025	·033	·032
Feb	—	—	—	—	—	—	—	—	—	·000	·003	·012	·018	·026	·024
Mar	—	—	—	—	—	—	—	—	—	—	·000	·009	·014	·022	·021
Apr	—	—	—	—	—	—	—	—	—	—	—	·000	·005	·013	·012
May	—	—	—	—	—	—	—	—	—	—	—	—	·000	·008	·007
June	—	—	—	—	—	—	—	—	—	—	—	—	—	·000	·000
July	—	—	—	—	—	—	—	—	—	—	—	—	—	—	·000

Retail prices index

	Jan	Feb	Mar	Apr	May	Jun
1982	78·73	78·76	79·44	81·04	81·62	81·85
1983	82·61	82·97	83·12	84·28	84·64	84·84
1984	86·84	87·20	87·48	88·64	88·97	89·20
1985	91·20	91·94	92·80	94·78	95·21	95·41
1986	96·25	96·60	96·73	97·67	97·85	97·79
1987	100·00	100·40	100·60	101·80	101·90	101·90
1988	103·30	103·70	104·10	105·80	106·20	106·60
1989	111·00	111·80	112·30	114·30	115·00	115·40
1990	119·50	120·20	121·40	125·10	126·20	126·70
1991	130·20	130·90	131·40	133·10	133·50	134·10
1992	135·60	136·30	136·70	138·80	139·30	139·30
1993	137·90	138·80	139·30	140·60	141·10	141·00
1994	141·30	142·10	142·50	144·20	144·70	144·70
1995	146·00	146·90	147·50	149·00	149·60	149·80
1996	150·20	150·90	151·50	152·60	152·90	153·00
1997	154·40	155·00	155·40	156·30	156·90	157·50
1998	159·50	160·30	160·80	162·60	163·50	163·40
1999	163·40	163·70	164·10	165·20	165·60	165·60
2000	166·60	167·50	168·40	170·10	170·70	171·10
2001	171·10	172·00	172·20	173·10	174·20	174·40
2002	173·30	173·80	174·50	175·70	176·20	176·20
2003	178·40	179·30	179·90	181·20	181·50	181·30
2004	183·10	183·80	184·60	185·70	186·50	186·80
2005	188·90	189·60	190·50	191·60	192·00	192·20
2006	193·40	194·20	195·00	196·50	197·70	198·50
2007	201·60	203·10	204·40	205·40	206·20	207·30
2008	209·80	211·40	212·10	214·00	215·19	216·80

	Jul	Aug	Sep	Oct	Nov	Dec
1982	81·88	81·90	81·85	82·26	82·66	82·51
1983	85·30	85·68	86·06	86·36	86·67	86·89
1984	89·10	89·94	90·11	90·67	90·95	90·87
1985	95·23	95·49	95·44	95·59	95·92	96·05
1986	97·52	97·82	98·30	98·45	99·29	99·62
1987	101·80	102·10	102·40	102·90	103·40	103·30
1988	106·70	107·90	108·40	109·50	110·00	110·30
1989	115·50	115·80	116·60	117·50	118·50	118·80
1990	126·80	128·10	129·30	130·30	130·00	129·90
1991	133·80	134·10	134·60	135·10	135·60	135·70
1992	138·80	138·90	139·40	139·90	139·70	139·20
1993	140·70	141·30	141·90	141·80	141·60	141·90
1994	144·00	144·70	145·00	145·20	145·30	146·00
1995	149·10	149·90	150·60	149·80	149·80	150·70
1996	152·40	153·10	153·80	153·80	153·90	154·40
1997	157·50	158·50	159·30	159·50	159·60	160·00
1998	163·00	163·70	164·40	164·50	164·40	164·40
1999	165·10	165·50	166·20	166·50	166·70	167·30
2000	170·50	170·50	171·70	171·60	172·10	172·20
2001	173·30	174·00	174·60	174·30	173·60	173·40
2002	175·90	176·40	177·60	177·90	178·20	178·50
2003	181·30	181·60	182·50	182·60	182·70	183·50
2004	186·80	187·40	188·10	188·60	189·00	189·90
2005	192·20	192·60	193·10	193·30	193·60	194·10
2006	198·50	199·20	200·10	200·40	201·10	202·70
2007	206·10	207·30	208·00	208·90	209·70	210·90
2008	216·50					

Corporation tax

Rates

Financial year	2003	2004	2005	2006	2007	2008
Full rate[4]	30%	30%	30%	30%	30%	28%
Starting rate	0%	0%	0%	–	–	–
first relevant amount[1]	£10,000	£10,000	£10,000	–	–	–
second relevant amount[1]	£50,000	£50,000	£50,000	–	–	–
marginal relief fraction	19/400	19/400	19/400	–	–	–
effective marginal rate[6]	23.75%	23.75%	23.75%	–	–	–
Small companies' rate[5]	19%	19%	19%	19%	20%	21%
lower relevant amount[1]	£300,000	£300,000	£300,000	£300,000	£300,000	£300,000
upper relevant amount[1]	£1.5m	£1.5m	£1.5m	£1.5m	£1.5m	£1.5m
marginal relief fraction	11/400	11/400	11/400	11/400	1/40	7/400
effective marginal rate[6]	32.75%	32.75%	32.75%	32.75%	32.50%	29.75%
Non-corporate distribution rate[2]	–	19%	19%	–	–	–
Tax credit: from 6 April[3]	10%	10%	10%	10%	10%	10%

[1] Reduced proportionally for accounting periods of less than 12 months. The limits are divided by the number of associated companies (including the company in question).

[2] Applies where the underlying corporation tax rate is lower than 19% (TA 1988 s 13AB, Sch A2).

[3] Individual shareholders not subject to higher rate tax have no further tax to pay. The abolition of the repayment of tax credit to charities was phased in over five years at 21% for 1999–2000, 17% for 2000–01, 13% for 2001–02, 8% for 2002–03 and 4% for 2003–04.

[4] For financial year 2009 the full rate of corporation tax will be 28%.

[5] The small companies rate will be 22% from 1 April 2009.

[6] For ring fenced trades, the small companies rate will remain at 19% for financial years 2007 and 2008 and the proposed change to both rates for 2009 will not apply.

Marginal relief. The starting and small companies' rate apply to *basic profits* ('I') where *profits* ('P') do not exceed the first or lower relevant amounts. Where *profits* ('P') exceed those amounts but not the second or upper relevant amounts, corporation tax on *basic profits* ('I') is reduced by (marginal relief upper profit limit – P) × I/P × fraction, where 'P' is profits as finally computed for corporation tax purposes *plus* franked investment income* excluding such income from UK companies in the same group or consortium of which the recipient is a member, 'I' is profits on which corporation tax is actually borne (income plus chargeable gains).

*Alternatively, where there is no franked investment income, apply starting or small companies rate up to first or lower relevant amount and effective marginal rates to balance of profits.

Reliefs

Corporate Venturing Scheme
(FA 2000 s 63, Schs 15, 16; FA 2001 s 64, Sch 16; FA 2004 s 95, Sch 20; FA 2006 s 91, Sch 14)
In relation to shares issued between 1 April 2000 and 31 March 2010, an investing company can obtain 20% CT relief on amounts subscribed for ordinary shares in small higher-risk unquoted trading companies which are held for at least three years. The investor must not own or be entitled to acquire more than 30% of the ordinary shares in the investee company. At least 20% must be owned by independent individuals. At least 80% of the investment must be employed wholly for the purpose of a relevant trade within 12 months. Chargeable gains on share disposals can be deferred by reinvestment in another shareholding. Allowable losses (net of 20% relief) can be set against income if not deducted from chargeable gains.

Research and development
(FA 2000 ss 68, 69, Schs 19–21; FA 2002 s 53, Sch 12; FA 2003 s 168, Sch 31; FA 2007 s 50)
An 'SME' incurring R&D expenditure of at least £10,000 (£25,000 for accounting periods beginning before 27 September 2003) in a 12-month accounting period can obtain relief for 150% of that expenditure. From 1 April 2002, large companies incurring R&D expenditure of at least £10,000 (£25,000 for accounting periods beginning before 9 April 2003) can obtain relief for 125% of that expenditure. Companies not yet in profit or which have not yet started to trade can claim relief upfront as a cash payment.
An 'SME' is a company with less than 500 employees (250 before 1 August 2008) and either annual turnover of €100m or less (€50m before 1 August 2008; £40m for accounting periods ending before 1 January 2005) or annual balance sheet total of €86m or less (€43m before 1 August 2008; £27m for accounting periods ending before 1 January 2005). From 1 April 2002, large companies incurring R&D expenditure of at least £10,000 (£25,000 for accounting periods beginning before 9 April 2003) can generally deduct 125% of the expenditure for SMEs . From 1 August 2008, the relief is to be increased to 175% of expenditure for SMEs and 130% for large companies. From the same date, relief for SMEs is to be limited to €7.5 per project.

Real Estate Investment Trusts (REITs)
(FA 2006 ss 103–145, Schs 16, 17)
From 1 January 2007, qualifying rental income from and gains on disposals of investment properties by UK companies within the REIT scheme will be exempt from corporation tax. See also p 47.
Community investment tax credit see p 62 **Urban regeneration companies** see p 62

Customs levies and taxes

Aggregates levy

(FA 2001 ss 16–49, Schs 4–10; SI 2004/1959)
Levy on commercial exploitation of aggregates including rock, gravel or sand together with any other substance incorporated or naturally occurring with it. Applies to all aggregate (not recycled) extracted in the UK or territorial waters unless exempt. It does not apply to quarried or mined products such as clay, shale, slate, metal and metal ores, gemstones, semi-precious gemstones and industrial minerals. It is charged at 20% of the full rate for aggregate processed in Northern Ireland until 31.3.2011.

1 April 2008 onwards	£1.95 per tonne
1 April 2002 to 31 March 2008	£1.60 per tonne

Climate change levy

(FA 2000 s 30, Sch 6; FA 2006 ss 171, 172; FA 2007 s 13)
Levy on supply for industrial or commercial purposes of energy, from 1.4.01, in the form of electricity, gas, petroleum and hydrocarbon gas supplied in a liquid state, coal and lignite, coke and semi-coke of coal or lignite and petroleum coke.

Taxable commodity supplied	Rate[1]		
	1.4.01–31.3.07	1.4.07–31.3.08	From 1 April 2008
Electricity	0.43p per kWh	0.441p per kWh	0.456p per kWh
Gas supplied by a gas utility or any gas supplied in a gaseous state that is of a kind supplied by a gas utility	0.15p per kWh	0.154p per kWh	0.159p per kWh
Any petroleum gas, or other gaseous hydrocarbon supplied in a liquid state	0.96p per kg	0.985p per kg	1.018p per kg
Any other taxable commodity	1.17p per kg	1.201p per kg	1.242p per kg

[1] Rate at which payable if supply is neither a half-rate supply nor a reduced-rate supply. The levy is charged at 20% of the full rate for energy-intensive users. It is charged at half the full rate for horticultural producers until 31.3.06. Horticultural businesses which sign climate change agreements can benefit from an 80% reduction in the levy in exchange for meeting specific energy efficiency targets.

Insurance premium tax

(FA 1994 ss 48–74, Schs 6A, 7, 7A)
IPT is a tax on premiums received under insurance contracts other than those which are specifically exempt.

	Standard rate	Higher rate[1]
From 1.7.99	5.0%	17.5%
1.4.97–30.6.99	4.0%	17.5%
1.10.94–30.3.97	2.5%	–

[1] The higher rate applies to sales of motor cars, light vans and motorcycles, electrical or mechanical domestic appliances, and travel insurance.

Landfill tax

(FA 1996 ss 39–71, 197, Sch 5; SI 1996/1527; SI 1996/1528)
Tax on disposal of waste imposed on operators of landfill sites calculated by reference to the weight and type of waste deposited. Exemption applies to mining and quarrying waste, dredging waste, pet cemeteries, waste from reclamation of contaminated land and inert waste used to restore licensed landfill sites. The standard rate will be increased to £32 per tonne and the lower rate to £2.50 per tonne after 31.3.08.

Period	Active waste per tonne	Inert waste per tonne	Maximum credit[1]
1.4.08–31.3.09	£32	£2.50	6%
1.4.07–31.3.08	£24	£2	6.6%
1.4.06–31.3.07	£21	£2	6.7%
1.4.05–31.3.06	£18	£2	6.0%
1.4.04–31.3.05	£15	£2	6.8%
1.4.03–31.3.04	£14	£2	6.5%
1.4.02–31.3.03	£13	£2	20.0%
1.4.01–31.3.02	£12	£2	20.0%

[1] Tax credits are available to operators who make donations to environmental trusts of 90% of the donation to the maximum percentage above of the tax payable in a 12-month period.

Income tax

Starting, basic and higher rates

Band of taxable income £	Band £	Rate %	Tax £	Cumulative tax £
2008–09				
0–34,800	34,800	20	6,960.00	6,960.00
Over £34,800	–	40		
2007–08				
0–2,230	2,230	10	223.00	223.00
2,231–34,600	32,370	22	7,121.40	7,344.40
over 34,600	–	40	–	–
2006–07				
0–2,150	2,150	10	215.00	215.00
2,151–33,300	31,150	22	6,853.00	7,068.00
over 33,300	–	40	–	–
2005–06				
0–2,090	2,090	10	209.00	209.00
2,091–32,400	30,310	22	6,668.20	6,877.20
over 32,400	–	40	–	–
2004–05				
0–2,020	2,020	10	202.00	202.00
2,021–31,400	29,380	22	6,463.60	6,665.60
over 31,400	–	40	–	–
2003–04				
0–1,960	1,960	10	196.00	196.00
1,961–30,500	28,540	22	6,278.80	6,474.80
over 30,500	–	40	–	–

Taxation of savings: For 2007–08 and earlier years, savings income is chargeable at the rates of 10% (if within the starting rate band), 20% and/or 40% (TA 1988 s 1A; FA 2000 s 32). From 2008–09 onwards the starting rate band is abolished. A new starting rate for savings band for individuals is introduced. For 2008–09 the band is £2,320. Where an individual's non-savings income is less than the starting rate limit for savings, the savings income is taxable at the 10% starting rate for savings up to the limit. Where non-savings income exceeds the limit, the starting rate for savings does not apply. Savings income includes interest from banks and building societies, interest distributions from authorised unit trusts, interest on gilts and other securities including corporate bonds, purchased life annuities and discounts. Where income does not exceed the basic rate limit, there will be no further tax to pay on savings income from which the 20% tax rate has been deducted, and any tax over-deducted is repayable. Higher rate taxpayers are liable to pay tax at 40% on that part of their savings income falling above the higher rate limit. Savings income is generally treated as the second top slice of income behind dividends. Non-taxpayers may apply to have interest paid without deduction of tax where their total income is expected to be covered by personal allowances. Taxpayers who are entitled to a refund of tax deducted from interest can claim the refund using form R40. HMRC have a *Taxback* website page to simplify repayments: www.hmrc.gov.uk/taxback.

Taxation of dividends: UK and foreign dividends (except those foreign dividends taxed under the remittance basis) form the top slice of taxable income. Where income does not exceed the basic rate limit the rate is 10% (applied to the dividend grossed-up by a tax credit of 1/9) so that the liability is met by the tax credit. Higher rate taxpayers are liable to pay tax at 32.5% on that part of their dividend income falling above the higher rate limit. See TA 1988 s 1A.

Real Estate Investment Trusts (REITs): From 1 January 2007, distributions paid out of tax exempt property income or gains by UK companies within the REIT scheme are treated as UK property income rather than dividends in the hands of investors and are paid under deduction of basic rate income tax.

Construction industry sub-contractors rate of deduction at source (from 6 April 2007): (SI 2007 No 46)

Registered sub-contractors	20%
Unregistered sub-contractors	30%

Taxation of trusts

	Rate applicable to trusts	Dividend trust rate
From 2004–05 onwards	40%	32.5%
1999–2000 to 2003–04	34%	25%

From 2005–06 onwards: The first £1,000 for 2006–07 onwards and £500 for 2005–06 of income arising to a trust chargeable at the rate applicable to trusts or the dividend trust rate is instead chargeable at the basic, savings or dividend rate depending on the type of income (ITA 2007 ss 9, 479–483, 491).

Vulnerable beneficiaries: From 2004–05 onwards, trustees can be taxed (on election) on trust income as if it were income of the vulnerable beneficiary taking into account the beneficiary's personal allowances, starting and basic rate bands (FA 2005 ss 23–45).

Table of income tax reliefs

	2008–09	2007–08
	£	£
Personal allowance (age under 65)	6,035	5,225
Age allowance[1]		
Total income limit	21,800	20,900
Personal allowance age 65–74	9,030	7,550
Not beneficial if individual's		
total income exceeds	27,790	25,550
Personal allowance age 75 and over	9,180	7,690
Not beneficial if individual's		
total income exceeds	28, 090	25,830
Married couple's allowance[2,4]		
Elder partner 65 before 6.4.2000		
Basic allowance	2,540	2,440
Age allowance[3,4]		
Total income limit	21,800	20,900
Neither partner aged 75 or over	6,535	6,285
Not beneficial if relevant partner[3]		
under 65 and his total income exceeds	29,790	28,590
65–74 and his total income exceeds	35,780	33,240
Either partner aged 75 and over	6,625	6,365
Not beneficial if relevant partner[3]		
under 65 and his total income exceeds	29,970	28,750
65–74 and his total income exceeds	35,960	33,400
75 or over and his total income exceeds	36,260	33,680
Children's tax credit[5]	–	–
Baby rate[6]	–	–
Blind person's allowance[7]	1,800	1,730

[1] The higher age allowances are available if the claimant's total income does not exceed the statutory income limit.

Where the total income exceeds the statutory limit, the maximum allowance is reduced by one-half of the excess until it is reduced to the ordinary personal allowance.

[2] The universal married couple's allowance was withdrawn for 2000–01 onwards but continues to be available to any married couple or, from 2005–06, civil partnership where at least one spouse or partner was born before 6 April 1935.

The relief is given as a reduction in income tax liability restricted to the lower of 10% of the amount of the allowance or the claimant's total income tax liability.

[3] The higher age allowances are available if the claimant's total income does not exceed the statutory income limit (subject to relief given as a reduction in tax liability as in note 2 above).

Where the total income exceeds the statutory limit, the maximum allowance is reduced by one-half of the excess (less any reduction made in the personal age allowance as in note 1 above) but it cannot be reduced to less than the basic couple's allowance.

National insurance contributions – self employed

Class 2	Flat rate per week	£2.30	£2.20
	Small earnings exception	4,825	4,635
Class 4	Band	5,435–40,040	5,225–34,840
	Rate	34,605@8%	29,615@8%
	Amount payable to upper limit	2,768.40	2,369.20
	Charge on profits above the limit	1%	1%

Table of income tax reliefs (cont.)

2006–07	2005–06	2004–05	2003–04	2002–03
£	£	£	£	£
5,035	4,895	4,745	4,615	4,615
20,100	19,500	18,900	18,300	17,900
7,280	7,090	6,830	6,610	6,100
24,590	23,890	23,070	22,290	20,870
7,420	7,220	6,950	6,720	6,370
24,870	24,150	23,310	22,510	21,410
2,350	2,280	2,210	2,150	2,110
20,100	19,500	18,900	18,300	17,900
6,065	5,905	5,725	5,565	5,465
27,530	26,750	25,930	25,130	24,610
32,020	31,140	30,100	29,120	27,580
6,135	5,975	5,795	5,635	5,535
27,670	26,890	26,070	25,270	24,750
32,160	31,280	30,240	29,260	27,720
32,440	31,540	30,480	29,480	28,260
–	–	–	–	5,290
–	–	–	–	10,490
1,660	1,610	1,560	1,510	1,480

4   For marriages entered into before 5 December 2005, married couple's allowance is given to the husband (subject to right of transfer to the wife), the amount of the allowance being determined by the level of the husband's income. For marriages and civil partnerships entered into on or after that date, the allowance is given to whichever of the two partners has the higher total income for the tax year in question, the amount of the allowance being determined by the level of that partner's income (subject to the right to transfer half or all of the basic allowance or excess allowances to the partner). Couples married before 5 December 2005 may make a joint election to be brought within the above rules for couples marrying on or after that date. The election must be made before the start of the first tax year for which it is to have effect. It will continue to have effect for all subsequent tax years and is irrevocable.

5   The relief is given as a deduction in the tax liability. It is withdrawn at the rate of £2 for every £3 of income chargeable to tax at the higher rate and is restricted to 10% of the resulting figure. From 2003–04 onwards, the relief was replaced by the Child Tax Credit.

6   For 2002–03 the amount per claimant is higher for the year of birth.

7   The allowance is available for persons who are registered blind but not for persons registered partially-sighted.

National insurance contributions – self employed (cont.)

£2.10	£2.10	£2.05	£2.00	£2.00
4,465	4,345	4,215	4,095	4,025
5,035–33,540	4,895–32,760	4,745–31,720	4,615–30,940	4,615–30,420
28,505@8%	27,865@8%	25,975@8%	26,325@8%	25,805@7%
2,280.40	2,229.20	2,158.00	2,106.00	1,806.35
1%	1%	1%	1%	–

Cars, vans and related benefits

Cars

From 6 April 2002: The income tax charge is based on a percentage of the car's price graduated according to the level of the car's carbon dioxide measured in grams per kilometre (g/km) and rounded down to the nearest 5g/km: ITEPA 2003 ss 114–148, 169; FA 2003 s 138. From 6 April 2008, there will be a 2% discount from the appropriate percentage rate for cars that have been manufactured to run on E85 fuel.

CO$_2$ emissions in grams per kilometre				% of list price	
2003–04	2004–05	2005–06– 2007–08	2008–09	Petrol	Diesel[1]
N/A	N/A	N/A	120	10%	13%
155	145	140	135	15%	18%
160	150	145	140	16%	19%
165	155	150	145	17%	20%
170	160	155	150	18%	21%
175	165	160	155	19%	22%
180	170	165	160	20%	23%
185	175	170	165	21%	24%
190	180	175	170	22%	25%
195	185	180	175	23%	26%
200	190	185	180	24%	27%
205	195	190	185	25%	28%
210	200	195	190	26%	29%
215	205	200	195	27%	30%
220	210	205	200	28%	31%
225	215	210	205	29%	32%
230	220	215	210	30%	33%
235	225	220	215	31%	34%
240	230	225	220	32%	35%
245	235	230	225	33%	35%
250	240	235	230	34%	35%
255	245	240	235	35%	35%

For 2008–09 onwards: For cars registered on or after 1.1.08 which are constructed to be capable of being propelled by bioethanol or E85 fuel, the percentage chargeable is reduced by 2%.
Where a car's CO$_2$ figure is not a multiple of 5, it is rounded down to the nearest 5. For 2008–09, however, a car's emissions figure must be exactly 120g/km or less to qualify for the 10%/13% rate.

Cars registered after 28 February 2001

For cars registered on or after 1.3.01, the definitive CO$_2$ emissions figure is recorded on the vehicle registration document. For cars first registered between 1.1.98 and 28.2.01, the Vehicle Certification Agency supply relevant information on their website at www.vcacarfueldata.org.uk and in their free, twice-yearly edition of the 'New Car Fuel Consumption & Emission Figures' booklet.

Cars registered on or after 1 January 1998 with no CO$_2$ emission figures

Cylinder capacity of car	Appropriate percentage[1]
1,400cc or less	15%
Over 1,400cc up to 2,000cc	25%
Over 2,000cc	35%
Electrically propelled vehicle	15%

[1] **Diesel cars:** A 3% supplement applies to diesel cars up to a maximum of 35%. The supplement does not apply to diesel cars meeting the Euro IV emissions standards until 5 April 2006 after which time it will apply to such cars registered on or after 1.1.06.

[2] **Discounts:** Special discounts apply to cars, with or without CO$_2$ emission figures, registered on or after 1.1.98: 6% for electrically propelled vehicles, 3% for hybrid electric vehicles (2% before 2006–07) and 2% for gas or bi-fuel cars with CO$_2$ emission figures for gas (1% before 2006–07).

Cars registered before 1.1.98 with no CO$_2$ emission figures: Tax is charged on 15% of the list price for engines to 1,400cc, 22% for engines of 1,401 to 2,000cc and 32% for engines above 2,000cc. Cars without a cylinder capacity are taxed on 32% of the list price (15% for electric cars).

List price of car:
(1) Includes any optional accessories supplied with the car when first made available to the employee and any further accessories costing £100 or more (ITEPA 2003 ss 122–131).
(2) Reduced by capital contributions made by the employee (maximum of £5,000) (ITEPA 2003 s 132).
(3) Capped at £80,000 (ITEPA 2003 s 121).
(4) Classic cars (aged 15 years or more and with a market value of £15,000 or more at the end of the year of assessment): substitute market value at end of year of assessment if this is higher than the adjusted list price. £80,000 cap and reduction for capital contributions apply (ITEPA 2003 s 147).

Automatic cars for disabled drivers: CO_2 figure reduced to equivalent for manual car (ITEPA 2003 s 138).

Car unavailable for part of year: Value of the benefit is reduced proportionately (ITEPA 2003 s 143).

National Insurance: Also used to calculate the national insurance contributions payable by employers on the benefit of cars they provide for the private use of their employees, see p 79.

1999–2000 to 2001–02: The income tax charge is based on cash equivalent of a percentage of the car's list price (see below) according to amount of business mileage.

Business miles	Car's age at end of tax year	
	Under 4 years	4 years or more
	% of list price	
Less than 2,500	35	26.25
2,500 but less than 18,000	25	18.75
18,000 or more	15	11.25

The cash equivalent is reduced proportionately where the car is not available for the whole tax year. The amount (as so reduced) is reduced by any payments made by the employee for private use.

List price of car:
(1) Includes qualifying accessories, excluding accessories provided after car made available if its list price was less than £100. Accessories designed for use only by disabled people also excluded. Where a car is manufactured so as to be capable of running on road fuel gas, its price is proportionately reduced by so much of that price as is reasonably attributable to it being manufactured in that way. Where a new car is converted to run on road fuel gas, the equipment is not regarded as an accessory.
(2) Reduced by capital contributions made by employee up to £5,000.
(3) List price as adjusted capped at £80,000.
(4) Classic cars (aged 15 years or more and with a market value of £15,000 or more at end of tax year): substitute market value at end of tax year if higher than adjusted list price. £80,000 cap and reduction for capital contributions apply.
(5) Mileage figures are reduced proportionately where car is not available for whole year.
(6) For second and subsequent cars there is no reduction if business mileage is under 18,000 miles; **from 1999–2000** reduce basic cash equivalent to 25% if business mileage is 18,000 miles or more.

Vans

(ITEPA 2003 ss 114–118, 154–166, 168, 169A, 170)

	Van's age at end of tax year	
	Under 4 years	4 years or more
2007–08 to 2008–09		
Vehicle weight up to 3,500kg	**£3,000**	**£3,000**
1993–94 to 2006–07:		
Vehicle weight up to 3,500kg	£500	£350

The charge also covers provision of fuel where there is unrestricted private use.

From 6 April 2005 no charge applies to employees who have to take their van home and private use is restricted other than for ordinary commuting (insignificant use is disregarded).

From 6 April 2007 the scale charge increased to £3,000 irrespective of the age of the van. An additional fuel charge of £500 will also apply for unrestricted private use (FA 2004 s 80, Sch 14).

Related benefits

Parking facilities: No taxable benefit for work place provision of car parking spaces, or parking for bicycles or motorcycles or, from 6 April 2005, vans (ITEPA 2003 s 237).

Cycles and cyclist's safety equipment: No taxable benefit in respect of the provision to employees of bicycles or cycling safety equipment for travel to and from work (ITEPA 2003 s 244) nor, from 6 April 2005, for subsequent transfer to the employee at market value (ITEPA 2003 s 206).

On-call emergency vehicles: From 6 April 2004 onwards no tax or NIC charge where emergency service workers have private use of their emergency vehicle when on call (ITEPA 2003 s 248A).

Bus services: From 6 April 2002 onwards no taxable benefit in respect of the provision of works buses with a seating capacity of nine or more provided to employees (or their children) to travel to and from work (ITEPA 2003 s 242).

Car and motorcycle hire: restricted allowances

(TA 1988 ss 578A, 578B; ITTOIA 2005 ss 48–50)

If a car with a retail price when new of more than £12,000 is acquired under a rental lease the maximum allowable deduction in computing trading profits is restricted to:

$$\frac{£12,000 + P}{2P} \times R$$

P = retail price of car when new. R = annual rental.

Capital allowances see p 23.

Car fuel: company cars

(ITEPA 2003 ss 149–153; TA 1988 s 158)
For 2003–04 onwards, the same percentage figures on p 50 used to calculate the car benefit charge for the company car, which are directly linked to the car's CO_2 emissions, are used to calculate the benefit charge for fuel provided for private motoring. The relevant percentage figure is multiplied by £14,400 for 2003–04 to 2007–08 and by £16,900 for 2008–09.

CO_2 emissions grams per kilometre	Petrol	Diesel
2008–09	**£**	**£**
120	1,690	2,197
135	2,535	3,042
140	2,704	3,211
145	2,873	3,380
150	3,042	3,549
155	3,211	3,718
160	3,380	3,887
165	3,549	4,056
170	3,718	4,225
175	3,887	4,394
180	4,056	4,563
185	4,225	4,732
190	4,394	4,901
195	4,563	5,070
200	4,732	5,239
205	4,901	5,408
210	5,070	5,577
215	5,239	5,746
220	5,408	5,915
225	5,577	5,915
230	5,746	5,915
235	5,915	5,915

CO_2 emissions grams per kilometre			Petrol	Diesel
2003–04	2004–05	2005–06 to 2007–08	£	£
155	145	**140**	2,160	2,592
160	150	**145**	2,304	2,736
165	155	**150**	2,448	2,880
170	160	**155**	2,592	3,024
175	165	**160**	2,736	3,168
180	170	**165**	2,880	3,312
185	175	**170**	3,024	3,456
190	180	**175**	3,168	3,600
195	185	**180**	3,312	3,744
200	190	**185**	3,456	3,888
205	195	**190**	3,600	4,032
210	200	**195**	3,744	4,176
215	205	**200**	3,888	4,320
220	210	**205**	4,032	4,464
225	215	**210**	4,176	4,608
230	220	**215**	4,320	4,752
235	225	**220**	4,464	4,896
240	230	**225**	4,608	5,040
245	235	**230**	4,752	5,040
250	240	**235**	4,896	5,040
255	245	**240**	5,040	5,040

The benefit is reduced to nil if the employee is required to, and does, make good all fuel provided for private use. There is no taxable benefit where the employer only provides fuel for business travel. From 2003–04, the charge is proportionately reduced where the employee stops receiving free fuel part way through the tax year, but where free fuel is subsequently provided in the same tax year, the full year's charge is payable. The benefit is proportionately reduced where a car is not available or is incapable of being used for part of a year (being at least 30 days).

2002–03		
Cylinder capacity:	1,400cc or less	£2,240
(non-diesel cars)	Over 1,400cc up to 2,000cc	£2,850
	Over 2,000cc	£4,200
Cylinder capacity:	2,000cc or less	£2,850
(diesel cars)	Over 2,000cc	£4,200
No internal combustion engine		£4,200
2001–02		
Cylinder capacity:	1,400cc or less	£1,930
(non-diesel cars)	Over 1,400cc up to 2,000cc	£2,460
	Over 2,000cc	£3,620
Cylinder capacity:	2,000cc or less	£2,460
(diesel cars)	Over 2,000cc	£3,620
No internal combustion engine		£3,620

Mileage allowances

Advisory fuel rates for company cars

Engine size	Cost per mile		
	Petrol	Diesel	LPG
from 1 July 2008			
1,400cc or less	12p	13p	7p
1,401–2,000cc	15p	13p	9p
Over 2,000cc	21p	17p	13p
from 1 January 2008			
1,400cc or less	11p	11p	7p
1,401–2,000cc	13p	11p	8p
Over 2,000cc	19p	14p	11p
1 August 2007–31 December 2007			
1,400cc or less	10p	10p	6p
1,401–2,000cc	13p	10p	8p
Over 2,000cc	18p	13p	10p
1 February 2007–31 July 2007			
1,400cc or less	9p	9p	6p
1,401–2,000cc	11p	9p	7p
Over 2,000cc	16p	12p	10p
1 July 2006–31 January 2007			
1,400cc or less	11p	10p	7p
1,401–2,000cc	13p	10p	8p
Over 2,000cc	18p	14p	11p
1.7.05–30.6.06			
1,400cc or less	10p	9p	7p
1,401–2,000cc	12p	9p	8p
Over 2,000cc	16p	13p	10p
6.4.04–30.6.05			
1,400cc or less	10p	9p	7p
1,401–2,000cc	12p	9p	8p
Over 2,000cc	14p	12p	10p

[1] Advisory fuel rates can be used to negotiate dispensations for mileage payments from 28 January 2002 where:
(a) employers reimburse employees for business travel in their company cars; or
(b) employers require employees to repay the cost of fuel used for private travel.

(In the case of (b) the figures may be used for reimbursements of private travel from 6 April 2001.)
[2] Payments at or below these rates are tax and NIC free. The table figures will be accepted for VAT purposes.
[3] Other rates may be used if the employer can demonstrate that they are justified.
[4] Rates are reviewed by HMRC every six months.
[5] The 1 July 2008 rates can be used from 1 June 2008 if the employer wishes.

Authorised mileage rates

	Rate per business mile	
Cars		
2002–03 onwards[1]	First 10,000 miles	Over 10,000 miles
2001–02[2]	**40p**	**25p**
Engine size	First 4,000 miles	Over 4,000 miles
Up to 1,500cc	40p	25p
1,501–2,000cc	45p	25p
Over 2,000cc	63p	36p
Fixed rate	42.5p	25p
Car passengers		
Allowance for each fellow passenger carried		
2002–03 onwards[1]		**5p**
Cycles and motorcycles	Cycles	Motorcycles
2002–03 onwards[1]	**20p**	**24p**
2000–01–2001–02	12p	24p

[1] Where the employer pays less than the authorised rate the employee can claim tax relief for the difference (ITEPA ss 229–232, 235, 236).

[2] Up to 2001–02, simplified arrangements could be operated known as the Fixed Profit Car Scheme (FPCS) or the Car Allowances Enhanced Reporting Scheme (CAERS), under which an employee's taxable business mileage profit was determined by reference to the engine size and the excess of the mileage allowance paid over the authorised rates.

Charities

Gift Aid scheme

Under the Gift Aid scheme an individual donor can claim higher rate relief on the grossed up amount of a monetary donation against income tax and capital gains tax. The charity claims basic rate relief on the grossed up amount of the donation. Donors must make a declaration that they are UK taxpayers to allow the charity to reclaim the repayment. One declaration can cover a series of donations to the same charity and the declaration can be made by writing, by electronic means or orally. A declaration can be backdated for up to six years prior to the declaration for donations made after 5 April 2000. The basic rate tax deemed to have been deducted by the donor at source is clawed back if the donor's tax liability is insufficient to match it. Following the reduction of the basic rate to 20% for 2008–09 onwards, a transitional relief supplement of 2% of grossed up qualifying donations is payable to charities for 2008–09 to 2010–11.

Donors may elect in their self-assessment tax returns for donations made after 5 April 2003 to be treated as made in the preceding tax year for higher rate relief purposes. From April 2004, taxpayers can nominate a charity to receive all or part of any tax repayment due to them. The nomination is made on the taxpayer's self-assessment tax return for 2003–04 and later years, with an indication of whether Gift Aid should apply to the donation.

From 6 April 2002, the scheme is extended to gifts to Community Amateur Sports Clubs.

Relief for payments falling due after 5 April 2000 under charitable covenants is given under the Gift Aid scheme.

(*ITA 2007 ss 413–430*)

Gifts in kind

Relief is available for gifts by companies to charities, community amateur sports clubs or educational establishments of goods produced or sold or of plant or machinery used for the purposes of the trade (TA 1988 ss 83A, 84; CAA 2001 s 63(2)–(4); ITTOIA 2005 ss 107–109; FA 2002 Sch 18 para 9(3)).

Gifts of land, shares and securities etc

Relief is available where a person disposes of listed shares and securities, unit trust units, AIM shares, etc or of freehold or leasehold interests in land to a charity by way of a gift or sale at an undervalue. The amount deductible from total income is the market value of the shares etc on the date of disposal plus incidental disposal costs less any consideration or value of benefits received by the donor or a connected person. This is in addition to any capital gains tax relief (ITA 2007, ss 431–446).

Payroll giving

Under the payroll giving scheme, employees authorise their employer to deduct charitable donations from their pay and receive tax relief on their donation at their top rate of tax. The government added a supplement to donations from 6 April 2000 to 5 April 2004. From 6 April 2004 to 31 December 2006, the first £10 donated by each employee every month will be matched for a period of six months. (FA 2000 s 38; FA 2003 s 148; ITEPA 2003 ss 713–715; SI 1986 No 2211).

Inheritance tax relief see p 74. **Capital gains tax** see p 29.

Employment benefits

The following benefits on pp 56 to 58 cover some common benefits not detailed separately elsewhere. References to 'lower-paid' employees are to those whose annual remuneration plus benefits is less than £8,500.

Accommodation, supplies, etc used in employment duties

(ITEPA 2003 s 316)
The provision of accommodation, supplies or services used by employees in performance of employment duties is not taxable provided:
- (a) if the benefit is provided on premises occupied by the employer, any private use by the employee (or the employee's family or household) is not significant; or
- (b) in any other case, the sole purpose of providing the benefit is to enable the employee to perform those duties, any private use is not significant and the benefit is not an excluded benefit (eg the provision of a motor vehicle, boat or aircraft).

Assets given to employees

(ITEPA 2003 ss 203, 204)
If new, tax is chargeable on the cost to the employer (market value in the case of a 'lower-paid' employee). If used, tax is chargeable on the greater of:
- (a) market value at the time of transfer; and
- (b) where the asset is first applied for the provision of a benefit after 5.4.80 and a person has been chargeable to tax on its use, market value when first so applied less amounts charged to tax for use up to and including the year of transfer.

Buses to shops

(SI 2002/205)
The provision of buses for journeys of ten miles or less from the workplace to shops etc on a working day is not taxable.

Cheap loans

(ITEPA 2003 ss 174–190)
A taxable benefit arises on employer-related loans to directors or employees earning £8,500 or more a year, on the difference between the interest paid and interest payable at the 'official rate' below. There is no tax charge where:
- (a) all the employer-related loans (or all loans not qualifying for tax relief) do not exceed £5,000;
- (b) all the interest payable is or would be eligible for tax relief; and
- (c) the loans are ordinary commercial loans.

The 'official rate' is:

From 6 April 2007	**6.25%**
From 6 January 2002 to 5 April 2007	5.00%
From 6 March 1999 to 5 January 2002	6.25%

The average rate for the tax year is:

2007–08	**6.25%**
2002–03 to 2006–07	5.00%
2001–2002	5.94%
1999–2000 to 2000–01	6.25%

From 2000–01 the official rate is set in advance for the whole of the following tax year, subject to review if the typical mortgage rates were to fall sharply during a tax year.

Christmas parties and annual functions

(ITEPA 2003 s 264; SI 2003/1361)
Not taxable if cost does not exceed £150 per head per tax year (£75 for 2002–03) and open to staff generally. Otherwise, fully taxable. Expenditure may be split between more than one function. (Not taxable on 'lower-paid' employees.)

Childcare provision

(ITEPA 2003 ss 318–318D; SI 2006/882)
From 2005–06, no liability arises:
- (a) where the premises (which are not wholly or mainly used as a private dwelling) are made available by the employer or, where the scheme is provided under arrangements with other persons, by one or more of those persons; or
- (b) where (a) does not apply, to the first £55 per week from 2006–07 or the first £50 per week for 2005–06 of registered or approved childcare.

Before 2005–06, broadly similar provisions to (a) applied.

Disabled employees

(ITEPA 2003 ss 246, 247; SI 2002/1596)
The provision of or payment for transport for disabled employees for ordinary commuting is tax free. From 9 July 2002, this also applies to the provision of equipment, services or facilities to disabled employees to help them carry out their duties of employment.

Eye tests and corrective appliances

(ITEPA 2003 s 320A; FA 2006 s 62)
From 2006–07, no liability arises where the provision of tests or special corrective appliances are required under health and safety legislation and are available as required to employees generally.

Homeworkers

(ITEPA 2003 s 316A)
From 2003–04, employer contributions to additional household costs not taxable where employee works at home. Supporting evidence required if contributions exceed £3 per week (£156 per year). Before 6 April 2008 the limit was £2 per week (£104 per year).

Incidental overnight expenses

(ITEPA 2003 ss 99–108)
Not taxable where employee stays away from home on business and payment from employer does not exceed:
- (a) £5 per night in the UK; or
- (b) £10 per night overseas.

Living accommodation

A taxable benefit (the '*basic charge*') arises on the annual rental value (or actual rent if greater) less any sums made good by the employee. There is an *additional charge* (if the basic charge is not calculated on the full open market rental value) where the cost of accommodation (including costs of any capital improvements less amounts made good by the employee) exceeds £75,000. The additional charge is the excess cost over £75,000 multiplied by the official rate for cheap loans (see above) in force at the start of the tax year less any rent paid by the employee in excess of the basic charge.
The charges are apportioned in the case of multiple occupation or if the property is provided for only part of the year or part is used exclusively for business purposes.
Exemption: No taxable benefit arises where living accommodation is provided:
- (a) for the proper performance of duties;
- (b) by reason that it is customary to do so; or
- (c) by reason of special threat to the employee's security.

The above exemptions apply to a full-time working director whose interest in the company does not exceed 5%, otherwise only exemption (c) applies to directors.

Living expenses

(ITEPA 2003 ss 313–315)
A taxable charge arises on the cost to the employer of the employee's living expenses. For the provision of assets such as furniture, see 'Use of employer's assets' on p 58.
Where the exemption for living accommodation above applies, the tax charge relating to living expenses (including the provision of furniture and items normal for domestic occupation) is restricted to 10% of the employee's net earnings from the related employment less any sums made good by the employee.
Expenditure on alteration and structural repairs which are normally the landlord's responsibility do not give rise to a taxable benefit.

Long service awards

(ITEPA 2003 s 323; SI 2003/1361)
Not taxable provided the employee has at least 20 years' service and cost to the employer does not exceed £50 (£20 where made before 13.6.03) for each year of service. No similar award may be made within ten years of such an award.

Meals

(ITEPA 2003 s 317)
Subsidised or free meals provided for staff generally at the workplace are not taxable.

Medical check-ups and insurance

(ITEPA 2003 s 325; HMRC Employment Income Manual EIM 21765)
2007–08 onwards: One screening and one check-up each year not taxable if available to all employees or, in the case of check-ups, available to all employees identified in a screening as needing a check-up (but note that for 2007–08 only, HMRC will not seek tax in respect of screenings or check-ups if they would not have been taxable under the previous rules).
2006–07 and earlier years: Routine health checks and medical screenings for employee (or members of the family or household) are not taxable. Insurance premiums paid on behalf of employees (other than 'lower-paid' employees) are taxable unless for treatment outside the UK whilst the employee is performing duties abroad.

Personal expenses

(ITEPA 2003 ss 70–72, 336–340)
Unless covered by specific exemptions, payments to an employee by reason of his employment in respect of expenses or allowances are taxable. Deduction is allowed for expenses the employee is obliged to incur which are:
- (a) qualifying travelling expenses (broadly those necessarily incurred other than for ordinary commuting or private travel); or
- (b) other amounts incurred wholly, exclusively and necessarily in the performance of employment duties.

Relocation expenses

(ITEPA 2003 ss 271–289)
Qualifying removal expenses and benefits up to £8,000 per move in connection with job-related residential moves are not taxable. Included are expenses of disposal, acquisition, abortive acquisition, transport of belongings, travelling and subsistence, bridging loans and duplicate expenses (replacement domestic items).

Third party gifts

(ITEPA 2003 ss 270, 324; SI 2003/1361)
Gifts during the tax year of goods and non-cash vouchers up to £250 (£150 for 2002–03) not taxable where provided by a party unconnected with the employer and not for services provided in connection with employment.

Use of employer's assets

(ITEPA 2003 ss 203–206, 242, 244, 320; FA 2005 s 17; FA 2006 ss 60, 61)
Tax is chargeable on the annual rental value of land and, for other assets, at 20% of the market value when they are first lent or the rental charge to the employer if higher. No taxable benefit arises on:
- (a) the loan of a mobile phone for private use (from 6 April 2006 this is restricted to one mobile phone per employee and no longer extends to the employee's family or household but phones first loaned before 6 April 2006 are not affected by the change);
- (b) the use of works buses (see p 51);
- (c) bicycles and cycle safety equipment (see p 51);
- (d) to 5 April 2006, the loan of computer equipment for private use, provided use is not restricted to directors or senior staff and value of benefit does not exceed £2,500 (computers made available for private use before 6 April 2006 are not affected by the change).
From 6 April 2005, no benefit arises on the subsequent purchase by an employee at market value of computer or cycling equipment previously on loan.

Vouchers

(ITEPA 2003 ss 73–89, 95, 96, 268–270, 362)
Vouchers are taxable as follows.

(a)	Cash vouchers	On amount for which voucher can be exchanged
(b)	Non-cash vouchers	On cost to employer less any contribution from employee (except where used to obtain certain non-taxable benefits)
(c)	Luncheon vouchers	On excess over 15p per working day
(d)	Transport vouchers	On cost to employer less any contribution from employee

Employment income

PAYE and national insurance thresholds

	2003–04	2004–05	2005–06	2006–07	2007–08	2008–09
	£	£	£	£	£	£
Weekly	89	91	94	97	100	105
Monthly	385	395	408	420	435	453

National minimum wage

(Hourly rate)

Age of worker	Under 18*	18–21**	22 or more
1.10.08–30.9.09	£3.53	£4.77	£5.73
1.10.07–30.9.08	£3.40	£4.60	£5.52
1.10.06–30.9.07	£3.30	£4.45	£5.35
1.10.05–30.9.06	£3.00	£4.25	£5.05
1.10.04–30.9.05	£3.00	£4.10	£4.85

* Applies to all workers under 18 who are no longer of compulsory school age.

** Also applies to workers aged 22 or more, starting a new job with a new employer, doing accredited training.

Basis of assessment

(ITEPA 2003 ss 14–43)

	Services performed			
Persons domiciled in UK	Wholly in UK	Partly in UK	Partly abroad	Wholly abroad
Non-resident	All	That part	None	None
Resident but not ordinarily resident	All	That part	Remittances	Remittances
Resident and ordinarily resident	All	All*	All*	All*
Persons domiciled outside the UK				
UK employer	As for person domiciled in the UK			
Foreign employer				
Non-resident	All UK earnings			
Resident but not ordinarily resident	All UK earnings and remittances for duties performed outside UK			
Resident and ordinarily resident	Remittances for duties performed outside UK			

* Exemption for seafarers if at least half of qualifying period of over 364 days worked abroad (including 183 consecutive days) (FA 1998 s 63; ITEPA 2003 ss 378–385).

Termination payments

The following lump sum payments are exempt from tax:
- (a) Payments in connection with the cessation of employment on the death, injury or disability of the employee.
- (b) Payments under unapproved retirement benefits schemes where the employee has been taxed on the actual or notional contributions to provide the benefit.
- (c) Payments under approved retirement benefits schemes which can properly be regarded as a benefit earned by past service.
- (d) Certain payments of terminal grants to members of the armed forces.
- (e) Certain benefits under superannuation schemes for civil servants in Commonwealth overseas territories.
- (f) Payments in respect of foreign service where the period of foreign service comprises:
  - (i) 75% of the whole period of service; or
  - (ii) the whole of the last 10 years of service; or
  - (iii) where the period of service exceeded 20 years, one-half of that period, including any 10 of the last 20 years.
- (g) Otherwise, a proportion of the payment is exempt, as follows:

$$\frac{\text{length of foreign service}}{\text{length of total service}} \times \text{amount otherwise chargeable}$$

- (h) The first £30,000 of genuine ex gratia payments (where there is no 'arrangement' by the employer to make the payment): (ITEPA 2003 ss 401–413).
- (i) Statutory redundancy payments (included in computing £30,000 limit in (g) above).

Fixed rate expenses

For most classes of industry fixed rate allowances for the upkeep of tools and special clothing have been agreed between HMRC and the trade unions concerned. Alternatively, the individual employee may claim as a deduction his or her actual expenses (ITEPA 2003 s 367). (HMRC Employment Income Manual, EIM 32712).

Industry	Occupation		Deduction from 2004–05 to 2007–08	Deduction from 2008–09
Agriculture	All workers[1]		70	100
Aluminium	(a)	Continual casting operators, process operators, de-dimplers, driers, drill punchers, dross unloaders, firemen[2], furnace operators and their helpers, leaders, mouldmen, pourers, remelt department labourers, roll flatteners	130	140
	(b)	Cable hands, case makers, labourers, mates, truck drivers and measurers, storekeepers	60	80
	(c)	Apprentices	45	60
	(d)	All other workers[1]	100	120
Banks and building societies	Uniformed doormen and messengers (£40 before 2004/05)		45	60
Brass and copper	Braziers, coppersmiths, finishers, fitters, moulders, turners and all other workers		100	120
Building	(a)	Joiners and carpenters	105	140
	(b)	Cement works, roofing felt and asphalt labourers	55	80
	(c)	Labourers and navvies (£40 before 2004/05)	45	60
	(d)	All other workers	85	120
Building materials	(a)	Stone masons	85	120
	(b)	Tilemakers and labourers (£40 before 2004/05)	45	60
	(c)	All other workers	55	80
Clothing	(a)	Lacemakers, hosiery bleachers, dyers, scourers and knitters, knitwear bleachers and dyers	45	60
	(b)	All other workers	45	60
Constructional engineering[3]	(a)	Blacksmiths and their strikers, burners, caulkers, chippers, drillers, erectors, fitters, holders up, markers off, platers, riggers, riveters, rivet heaters, scaffolders, sheeters, template workers, turners, welders	115	140
	(b)	Banksmen, labourers, shop-helpers, slewers, straighteners	60	80
	(c)	Apprentices and storekeepers	45	60
	(d)	All other workers	75	100
Electrical and electricity supply	(a)	Those workers incurring laundry costs only	45	60
	(b)	All other workers	90	120
Engineering (trades ancillary to)	(a)	Pattern makers	120	140
	(b)	Labourers, supervisory and unskilled workers	60	80
	(c)	Apprentices and storekeepers	45	60
	(d)	Motor mechanics in garage repair shops	100	120
	(e)	All other workers	100	120
Fire service	Uniformed firefighters and fire officers		60	80
Food	All workers		45	60
Forestry	All workers		70	100
Glass	All workers		60	80
Healthcare staff in the NHS, private hospitals and nursing homes	(a)	Ambulance staff on active service	110	140
	(b)	Nurses and midwives, chiropodists, dental nurses, occupational, speech and other therapists, phlebotomists and radiographers	70	100
	(c)	Plaster room orderlies, hospital porters, ward clerks, sterile supply workers, hospital domestics, hospital catering staff	60	100
	(d)	Laboratory staff, pharmacists, pharmacy assistants	45	60
	(e)	Uniformed ancillary staff: maintenance workers, grounds staff, drivers, parking attendants and security guards, receptionists and other uniformed staff	45	60
Heating	(a)	Pipe fitters and plumbers	100	120
	(b)	Coverers, laggers, domestic glaziers, heating engineers and their mates	90	120
	(c)	All gas workers, all other workers	70	100
Iron mining	(a)	Fillers, miners and underground workers	100	120
	(b)	All other workers	75	100

Industry	Occupation		Deduction from 2004–05 to 2007–08	Deduction from 2008–09
Iron and steel	(a)	Day labourers, general labourers, stockmen, time keepers, warehouse staff and weighmen	60	80
	(b)	Apprentices	45	60
	(c)	All other workers	120	140
Leather	(a)	Curriers (wet workers), fellmongering workers, tanning operatives (wet)	55	80
	(b)	All other workers (£40 before 2004/05)	45	60
Particular engineering[4]	(a)	Pattern makers	120	140
	(b)	Chainmakers, cleaners, galvanisers, tinners and wire drawers in the wire drawing industry, tool-makers in the lock making industry	100	120
	(c)	Apprentices and storekeepers	45	60
	(d)	All other workers	60	80
Police force		Uniformed police officers (ranks up to and including Chief Inspector) (£110 for 2007–08 only)	55	140
Precious metals		All workers	70	100
Printing	(a)	Letterpress section — electrical engineers (rotary presses), electrotypers, ink and roller makers, machine minders (rotary), maintenance engineers (rotary presses) and stereotypers	105	140
	(b)	Bench hands (periodical and bookbinding section), compositors (letterpress section), readers (letterpress section), telecommunications and electronic section wire room operators, warehousemen (paper box making section)	45	60
	(c)	All other workers	70	100
Prisons		Uniformed prison officers	55	80
Public service	(i)	Dock and inland waterways		
		(a) Dockers, dredger drivers, hopper steerers	55	80
		(b) All other workers (£40 before 2004/05)	45	60
	(ii)	Public transport		
		(a) Garage hands (including cleaners)	55	80
		(b) Conductors and drivers (£40 before 2004/05)	45	60
Quarrying		All workers	70	100
Railways		(See the appropriate category for craftsmen, eg engineers, vehicles etc.) All other workers	70	100
Seamen		Carpenters		
	(a)	Passenger liners	165	165
	(b)	Cargo vessels, tankers, coasters and ferries	130	140
Shipyards	(a)	Blacksmiths and their strikers, boilermakers, burners, carpenters, caulkers, drillers, furnacemen (platers), holders up, fitters, platers, plumbers, riveters, sheet iron workers, shipwrights, tubers, welders	115	140
	(b)	Labourers	60	80
	(c)	Apprentices and storekeepers	45	60
	(d)	All other workers	75	100
Textiles and textile printing	(a)	Carders, carding engineers, overlookers and technicians in spinning mills	85	120
	(b)	All other workers	60	80
Vehicles	(a)	Builders, railway vehicle repairers, and railway wagon lifters	105	140
	(b)	Railway vehicle painters and letterers, builders' and repairers' assistants	60	80
	(c)	All other workers	45	60
Wood & furniture	(a)	Carpenters, cabinet makers, joiners, wood carvers and wood-cutting machinists	115	140
	(b)	Artificial limb makers (other than in wood), organ builders and packing case makers	90	120
	(c)	Coopers not providing own tools, labourers, polishers and upholsterers	45	60
	(d)	All other workers	75	100

1   'All workers' and 'all other workers' refer only to manual workers who have to bear the cost of upkeep of tools and special clothing. They do not extend to other employees such as office staff.

2   'Firemen' means persons engaged to light and maintain furnaces.

3   'Constructional engineering' means engineering undertaken on a construction site, including buildings, shipyards, bridges, roads and other similar operations.

4   'Particular engineering' means engineering undertaken on a commercial basis in a factory or workshop for the purposes of producing components such as wire, springs, nails and locks.

Investment reliefs

Community investment tax credit

(ITA 2007 ss 333–382)
Investments made after 16 April 2002 by an individual or company in an accredited community development finance institution (CDFI) are eligible for tax relief up to 25%. The investment may be a loan or a subscription for shares or securities. Tax relief may be claimed for the tax year in which the investment is made and each of the four subsequent years. Relief for each year is the smaller of 5% of the invested amount, or the amount which reduces the investor's income tax liability for the year to nil.

Enterprise investment scheme

(ITA 2007 ss 156–257)
The EIS applies to investments in qualifying unquoted companies trading in the UK. Eligible shares must be held for at least three years from the issue date or commencement of trade if later (five years from the issue date for shares issued before 6 April 2000). The following reliefs apply subject to this and other conditions.

Relief on investment

Maximum investment:	From 2008–09	£500,000
	2006–07 to 2007–08	£400,000
	2004–05 to 2005–06	£200,000
	1998–99 to 2003–04	£150,000
Minimum investment:	From 1993–94	£500
Maximum carry-back to preceding year (up to 1/2 amount invested between 6 April and 5 October)	From 2006–07	£50,000
	1998–99 to 2005–06	£25,000
Rate of relief	From 1993–94	20%*

* Given as a deduction against income tax liability.

Other reliefs (TCGA 1992 ss 150A–150D, Schs 5B, 5BA)
  (a) A gain on a disposal of shares on which EIS relief has been given and not withdrawn is exempt from capital gains tax.
  (b) Deferral relief is available for gains on assets where the disposal proceeds are reinvested in eligible shares in a qualifying company one year before or three years after the disposal.
  (c) A loss on a disposal of shares on which EIS relief has been given may be relieved against income tax or capital gains tax.

Venture capital trusts

(ITA 2007 ss 258–332)
An individual who subscribes for ordinary shares in a VCT obtains income tax reliefs at the rates in the table below subject to conditions. The shares must be held for at least five years (three years for shares issued before 6 April 2006 and five years for shares issued before 6 April 2000).

Relief on investment

Maximum annual investment:	From 2004–05	£200,000
	1995–96 to 2003–04	£100,000
Rate of relief:	2006–07	30%
	2004–05 to 2005–06	40%
	1995–96 to 2003–04	20%

Other reliefs
  (a) Dividends on shares within investment limit exempt from income tax (unless the investor's main purpose is tax avoidance – from 9 March 1999).
  (b) Capital gains reliefs (see p 29).

Urban Regeneration Companies

Relief is available from 1 April 2003 for expenditure incurred by businesses in making contributions to designated Urban Regeneration Companies (TA 1988 s 79B; FA 2003 s 180; ITTOIA 2005 ss 82, 86).

Individual savings accounts ('ISAs')

(TA 1988 s 333; ITTOIA 2005 ss 694–701; SI 1998/1870; SI 2001/908)
Savers can subscribe to an ISA up to the following limits per tax year.

Overall annual subscription limit	1999–2000 to 2007–08	£7,000	**2008–09**	**£7,200**
Cash limit	1999–2000 to 2007–08	£3,000	**2008–09**	**£3,600**
Life insurance limit	1999–2000 to 2004–05	£1,000	**2008–09**	**N/A**

Before 2008–09 a limit of £4,000 (£3,000 before 2005–06) also applied to stocks and shares held in a mini-ISA. The limits are not affected by any TESSAs or PEPs held. The subscription limit applies to each spouse. Shares acquired under an approved share incentive plan, profit sharing scheme or SAYE option scheme may be transferred to a stocks and shares component of an ISA within 90 days without tax consequences. From 2008-09 PEP and TESSA accounts are transferred into ISA accounts

Reliefs
(a) Investments under the scheme are free from income tax and capital gains tax.
(b) 10% tax credit paid until 5 April 2004 on dividends from UK equities.
(c) Withdrawals may be made at any time without loss of tax relief.

Tax-exempt special savings accounts ('TESSAs')

(Accounts opened **before 6 April 1999:** TA 1988 ss 326A–326C)
From 2008-09, all TESSA accounts are transferred to ISA accounts.
Interest and bonuses received in the first five years (or on death if earlier) are exempt from income tax providing conditions are met. Withdrawals within the initial five-year period result in the loss of all tax exemption (including on interest already received). Interest earned after the maturity of the TESSA is taxable. Deposits could be made up to £3,000 in the first 12 months, £1,800 in any succeeding 12-month period and £9,000 in total.
Up to the full amount of the capital at maturity of a first TESSA could be invested in a follow-up TESSA within six months and similar conditions apply to a follow-up TESSA.
The capital in a TESSA opened before 6 April 1999 could, on maturity, be transferred to an ISA (see above). The capital in a TESSA that matured between 6 January 1999 and 5 April 1999 could be transferred into an ISA after 5 April 1999 if no follow-up TESSA was opened. Such transfers do not affect amounts which can be subscribed to an ISA.

Personal equity plans ('PEPs')

(Subscriptions made **before 6 April 1999**: TA 1988 s 333; SI 1989/469; SI 1998/1869)
From 2008–09, all PEP accounts are transferred to ISA accounts.
Before 6 April 1999, subscriptions to PEPs could be made up to a maximum per year of £6,000 to a general plan and £3,000 to a single company plan. Dividend income is tax free and a 10% tax credit was payable until 5 April 2004 on dividends from UK equities. Interest on cash held is paid gross and is tax free if reinvested.
PEPs held at 5 April 1999 can continue to be held with the same tax advantages as an ISA (see above) and without affecting the amount that can be subscribed to an ISA.

National Savings Bank interest

The first £70 of any interest you receive from a National Savings Ordinary Account is tax free. It is not possible to open a new Ordinary Account after 28 January 2004.

Miscellaneous reliefs

Foster carers

(ITTOIA 2005 ss 803–828)
Generally, local authority payments to foster carers are not taxable to the extent they do no more than meet the actual costs of caring. In other cases, for 2003–04 onwards:
- where gross receipts do not exceed the 'individual limit', the carer is treated as having a nil profit and nil loss for the tax year concerned;
- where gross receipts exceed the 'individual limit', the carer can choose to either be taxed on the excess or compute profit or loss using the normal business rules.

The 'individual limit' is made up of a fixed amount of £10,000 per residence for a full tax year plus an amount per child for each week or part week that the individual provides foster care. The weekly amounts are £200 for a child under 11 years and £250 for a child of 11 or over.

Landlord's energy-saving allowance

(ITTOIA 2005 ss 312–314, SI 2007/831)
From 6 April 2004 to 5 April 2015 individual landlords who let residential property and pay income tax may claim a deduction from the property business profits for expenditure in the dwelling-houses let to install:
- loft insulation or cavity wall insulation; or
- (from 7 April 2005) solid wall insulation; or
- (from 6 April 2006) draught-proofing and insulation for hot water systems; or
- (from 6 April 2007) floor insulation.

Expenditure is restricted to £1,500 per building until 5 April 2007 and to £1,500 per dwelling-house from 6 April 2007.
The relief it extended to corporate landlords of residential property for expenditure on or after 8 July 2008.

Life assurance premium relief

(TA 1988 s 266, Sch 14 para 7)
Relief for premiums paid on qualifying life assurance policies for contracts made before 14 March 1984 is available by deduction of 12.5% from admissible premiums.

Maintenance payments

(ITTOIA 2005 ss 727, 729; ITA 2007 ss 453–456)
Where either party to the marriage was born before 6 April 1935 tax relief may be claimed by the payer in respect of the lower of:
- the amount of the payments in the year concerned and
- the minimum amount of the married couple's allowance for the year concerned (see p 48).

The relief is restricted to 10% of the relevant amount. The payment must be made to the divorced or separated spouse. It is made gross and is not taxable in the hands of the recipient.

Rent-a-room relief

(ITTOIA 2005 ss 784–802; F(No 2)A 1982 Sch 10)
Gross annual receipts from letting furnished accommodation in the only or main home are exempt from tax up to a maximum of £4,250 (provided no other taxable income is derived from a trade, letting or arrangement from which the rent-a-room receipts are derived).
If the gross receipts exceed £4,250, the taxpayer can pay tax on the net receipts after deduction of expenses. Alternatively, the taxpayer can elect to pay tax on the amount by which the gross receipts exceed £4,250, without relief for the actual expenses.
An individual's maximum is halved to £2,125 if during the 'relevant period' for the year (normally the tax year) some other person received income from letting accommodation in that property.
An election can be made to disapply the relief for a particular tax year (for example, if the individual would otherwise make an allowable loss).

Pension provision from 6 April 2006

(FA 2004 ss 149–284, Schs 28–36)

From 6 April 2006, a new pension scheme tax regime fully replaces pre-existing rules for occupational pension schemes, personal (and stakeholder) pension schemes and retirement annuity schemes.

Tax relief on contributions

Individual contributions: Contributions to registered schemes are not limited by reference to a fraction of earnings and there is no earnings cap. There is no provision for the carry-back or carry-forward of contributions to tax years other than the year of payment.

An individual may make unlimited contributions and tax relief is available on contributions up to the higher of:

- the full amount of relevant earnings; or
- £3,600 provided the scheme operates tax relief at source.

Employer contributions: Employer contributions to registered schemes are deductible for tax purposes, with statutory provision for spreading abnormally large contributions over a period of up to four years. The contributions are not treated as taxable income of the employee.

Annual allowance

Each individual has an annual allowance as set out in the table below. If the annual increase in an individual's rights under all registered schemes exceeds the annual allowance, the excess is chargeable at 40%, the individual being liable for the tax.

Annual allowance	2006–07	2007–08	**2008–09**	2009–10	2010–11
	£215,000	£225,000	**£235,000**	£245,000	£255,000

Taxable benefits

'Tax-free' lump sum: The maximum 'tax-free' lump sum that can be paid to a member under a registered scheme is broadly the lower of:

- 25% of the value of the pension rights; and
- 25% of the member's lifetime allowance.

Lifetime allowance: Each individual has a lifetime allowance for contributions as set out in the table below. The excess over the lifetime allowance of the benefits crystallising (usually when a pension begins to be paid) is taxable at the following rates:

- 55% if taken as a lump sum;
- 25% in other cases.

Any tax due may be deducted from the individual's benefits.

Lifetime allowance	2006–07	2007–08	**2008–09**	2009–10	2010–11
	£1,500,000	£1,600,000	**£1,650,000**	£1,750,000	£1,800,000

Transitional. There are transitional provisions for the protection of lump sum and other pension rights accrued before 6 April 2006.

Age restrictions

Minimum pension age: The minimum pension age is 50 (rising to 55 on 6 April 2010). A pension cannot be paid before the minimum age except on grounds of ill health. Those with existing contractual rights to draw a pension earlier will have those rights protected and there is special protection for members of pre-6 April 2006 approved schemes with early retirement ages (see p 68). A reduced lifetime allowance will apply in the case of early retirement before age 50 except in the case of certain professions such as the police and the armed forces (to be prescribed by regulations).

Maximum benefit age: Benefits must be taken by the age of 75 at the latest. A member of a money purchase scheme may take a pension from the age of 75 by way of income withdrawal (known as an 'alternatively secured pension') instead of taking a scheme pension or purchasing a lifetime annuity. The maximum alternatively secured pension is 70% of a comparable annuity.

Personal pension schemes and retirement annuities

Provisions to 5 April 2006

1 July 1988 to 5 April 2006: Retirement annuity contracts were replaced by personal pension schemes, although retirement annuity premiums may continue to be paid, and tax relief obtained (TA 1988 ss 618–629). There are provisions for the carrying back (TA 1988 s 619) and the carrying forward (TA 1988 s 625) of relief, and these are not affected by FA 2000.

6 April 2001 to 5 April 2006: The personal pension scheme rules were adapted to accommodate the stakeholder pensions provisions (TA 1988 ss 630–655). From that date, personal pension and stakeholder pension contributions are subject to the same rules.

Tax relief on contributions

Retirement annuities: Premiums continue to be deducted from or set off against relevant earnings (TA 1988 s 619). The amount of relief available is based on a percentage of net relevant earnings (see maximum amount, below).

Personal pension schemes: Before 6 April 2001, premiums were deducted from or set off against relevant earnings (TA 1988 s 639, as enacted). The amount of relief available was based on a percentage of net relevant earnings (see maximum amount, below).

Personal pension schemes/stakeholder pensions:

Contributions not exceeding the earnings threshold
(1) Contributions of up to £3,600 gross ('the earnings threshold') may be paid into a stakeholder pension by anyone who is not a member of an occupational pension scheme, regardless of the amount (if any) of their earnings (TA 1988 s 632A).
(2) An individual who is a member of an occupational pension scheme but who is not a controlling director and whose total annual remuneration is no more than £30,000 is allowed to pay into both an occupational scheme and a stakeholder pension and will receive tax relief on an annual contribution of up to £3,600 (gross) into the stakeholder pension (TA 1988 s 632B).

Contributions exceeding the earnings threshold
(1) Contributions in excess of the earnings threshold may be made. Tax relief is given on contributions up to a maximum based on a percentage of net relevant earnings (see maximum percentage below).
(2) For the purpose of supporting contributions in excess of the earnings threshold, a tax year for which evidence of relevant earnings can be provided may be nominated as the basis year and contributions based on the amount of those earnings may be paid in each of the next five years (TA 1988 s 646B). The provisions enable an individual to make pension contributions for up to five years after the relevant earnings ceased, by reference to the net relevant earnings of a basis year which may be any one of the six tax years preceding the first year for which there are no relevant earnings (TA 1988 s 646D).

Carry-back of relief

Carry-back of relief is provided for in TA 1988 s 641A. There is no carry forward of relief (FA 2000 Sch 13 para 19).

Basic and higher rate relief

From 6 April 2001, contributions are payable net of basic rate tax relief. Tax relief at the higher rate is given by extending the basic rate band by the amount of the contribution paid in the year of assessment (TA 1988 s 639).

From 2001–02, relief for contributions is given up to a maximum which is the greater of:
(a) the 'earnings threshold'; and
(b) the 'maximum percentage' of net relevant earnings for the year (TA 1988 s 640, as amended by FA 2000 Sch 13 para 16).

For the purposes of calculating the maximum percentage, net relevant earnings are subject to an earnings cap (TA 1988 s 640A).

Maximum amount

Personal pension schemes/ stakeholder pensions (TA 1988 s 640)	Age in years at beginning of year of assessment	Maximum percentage
	35 and below	171/2
	36 to 45	20
	46 to 50	25
	51 to 55	30
	56 to 60	35
	61 or more	40
Earnings cap	£	
2005–06	105,600	
2004–05	102,000	
2003–04	99,000	
2002–03	97,200	
2001–02	95,400	
2000–01	91,800	
Retirement annuities (TA 1988 s 626)	Age in years at beginning of year of assessment	Maximum percentage
	50 and below	171/2
	51 to 55	20
	56 to 60	221/2
	61 or more	271/2

Life insurance element (TA 1988 s 640(3), as amended)

The maximum amount of contributions in respect of life insurance on which tax relief can be given is limited to a percentage of net relevant earnings (retirement annuities; personal pension contracts taken out before 6 April 2001) or of total amount of relevant pension contributions (personal pensions/stakeholder pension contracts taken out after 5 April 2001).

	Maximum percentage of net relevant earnings
Retirement annuities (contracts for dependants or life insurance)	5%
Personal pension schemes (contract of life insurance made before 6 April 2001)	5%
	Maximum percentage of total relevant pension contributions
Personal pension schemes/stakeholder pensions	
Contract of life insurance made after 5 April 2001	10%

Approval of contracts – early retirement ages

Trades and professions for which an early retirement age was agreed by the Revenue under TA 1988 s 620(4)(c) for the purpose of the approval of retirement annuity contracts are set out below. Under the personal and stakeholder pensions legislation, individuals may not take benefits from their pension arrangements before the age of 50. The trades and professions listed below for which the Revenue has approved an earlier retirement age of 30, 35, 40 or 45 have been approved under TA 1988 s 634(3)(b) for the purposes of personal pension schemes and stakeholder pensions. (See p 65 for minimum age restrictions.)

Retirement age	Profession or occupation		
30	downhill skiers		
35	athletes badminton players boxers cyclists dancers footballers	ice hockey players models national hunt jockeys rugby league players rugby union players squash players	table tennis players tennis players (including real tennis players) wrestlers
40	cricketers divers (saturation, deep sea and free swimming)	golfers motorcycle riders (motorcross or road racing) motor racing drivers	speedway drivers trapeze artists WPBSA snooker players
45	flat racing jockeys	members of the reserve forces	
50	circus animal trainers croupiers interdealer brokers martial arts instructors moneybroker dealers	off-shore riggers (mechanical fitters, pipe fitters, riggers, platers, welders and roustabouts) Royal Navy reservists	rugby league referees territorial army members TV newsreaders
55	air pilots brass instrumentalists distant water trawlermen firemen (part-time) health visitors (female)	inshore fishermen midwives (female) moneybroker dealer managers and directors responsible for dealers nurses (female) physiotherapists (female)	psychiatrists (who are also maximum part-time specialists employed within the NHS solely in the treatment of the mentally disordered) singers

Share schemes

Share incentive plans ('SIPs')

(TCGA 1992 ss 236A, 238A, Schs 7C, 7D Pt 1; ITEPA 2003 ss 488–515, Sch 2; FA 2003 s 139, Sch 21)
Applications for approval of Share Incentive Plans could be made from 28 July 2000.

Free share plan

2000–01 onwards	annual maximum	£3,000

Partnership share plan

2000–01 to 2002–03	monthly maximum	£125 or 10% of monthly salary if lower
2003–04 onwards	annual maximum	£1,500 or 10% of annual salary if lower

Matching shares

2000–01 onwards	Maximum number of shares given by employer to employee for each partnership share bought	2

Shares are free of tax and NICs if held in the plan for five years. Dividends up to £1,500 per employee per tax year are tax free if reinvested in shares. Shares withdrawn from the plan at any time are exempt from capital gains tax and are treated as acquired by the employee at their market value at that time.
If shares are withdrawn within between three and five years (with exceptions such as on death, disability, normal retirement or redundancy), liability to income tax and NICs arises on the lower of their value on entering and on leaving the plan. If shares are withdrawn within three years (with similar exceptions), liability is on their value on leaving the plan.

Enterprise management incentives

(TCGA 1992 s 238A, Sch 7D Pt 4; ITEPA 2003 ss 527–541, Sch 5)
Certain independent trading companies with gross assets not exceeding £30 million may grant share options then worth up to £120,000 (£100,000 for options granted before 6 April 2008) to an eligible employee. The total value of shares in respect of which unexercised qualifying options exist must not exceed £3 million. An additional restriction, limiting the scheme to companies with fewer than 250 full-time equivalent employees, is to be introduced with effect from the date FA 2008 receives Royal Assent.
Where the conditions of the scheme are complied with:
- (a) There is no charge to tax or NICs when the option is granted provided the option to acquire the shares is not at less than their market values at that date, and there is no charge on exercise providing the option is exercised within ten years.
- (b) Capital gains tax will be payable when the shares are sold, but business assets taper relief (see p 27) will be available and starts from the date on which the options are granted.

Approved save as you earn (SAYE) share option schemes

(TCGA 1992 s 238A, Sch 7D Pt 2; ITEPA 2003 ss 516–520, Sch 3; FA 2003 s 139, Sch 21)
The scheme is linked to an approved savings scheme, on which bonuses are exempt from tax, to provide funds for the acquisition of shares when the option is exercised at the end of a three or five-year contract. A five-year contract may offer the option of repayment on the seventh anniversary.

Monthly contributions to SAYE scheme

Minimum	£5–£10[1]
Maximum	£250

[1] The company may choose a minimum savings contribution between £5 and £10.

See the Treasury website (www.hm-treasury.gov.uk) for the bonus rates.
Where the conditions of the scheme are complied with, no income tax charge arises on the employee in respect of:
- (a) the grant of an option to acquire shares at a discount of up to 20% of the share price at time of the grant;
- (b) the exercise of the option (options must not be exercised before the bonus date subject to cessation of employment due to injury, disability, redundancy, retirement or death); or
- (c) any increase in the value of the shares.
Capital gains tax is chargeable on disposal of the shares: the CGT base cost is the consideration given by the employee for both the shares and the option.

Company share option plans ('CSOPs')

(TCGA 1992 s 238A, Sch 7D Pt 3; ITEPA 2003 ss 521–526, Sch 4; FA 2003 s 139, Sch 21)

Limit on value of shares under option held by employee at any one time

From 29 April 1996	£30,000

Scheme shares must be fully paid up, not redeemable and not subject to special restrictions. Only full-time directors or qualifying employees may participate in the scheme.

Where the conditions of the scheme are complied with, no tax charge arises on the employee in respect of:
- (a) the grant of an option to acquire shares[1];
- (b) the exercise of the option[2]; or
- (c) any increase in the value of the shares.

Capital gains tax is chargeable on disposal of the shares: the CGT base cost is the consideration given by the employee for both the shares and the option.

[1] At the time the option is granted the price at which shares can be acquired must not be less than the market value of shares of the same class at that time.

[2] The option must be exercised between three and ten years after the grant (or may be exercised less than three years after the grant where the individual ceases to be an employee due to injury, disablement, redundancy or retirement). For options granted before 9 April 2003, the options must be exercised between three and ten years after the grant (without exception) and not less than three years after a previous exempt exercise of another option under the same or another approved company share option scheme.

Approved profit sharing schemes

(TA 1988 ss 186, 187, Schs 9, 10)

NOTE: The income tax relief in respect of awards of shares under approved profit sharing schemes was withdrawn for awards of shares made after 31 December 2002: FA 2000 s 49.

Annual limit on shares appropriated

From 1991–92	Greater of £3,000 or 10% of salary, up to £8,000

Schedule E charge on early disposal or receipt of capital from shares

Time of disposal or capital receipt	Percentage charge[1]
Before third anniversary of appropriation	100%[2]

[1] Calculated on the appropriate percentage of the initial market value of the shares when appropriated (or the sales proceeds if less).

[2] The charge is reduced to 50% where the employee reaches the retirement age specified in the scheme rules or leaves the employment due to injury, disability or redundancy before the shares are sold or capital is received.

Where the conditions of the scheme are satisfied, no tax charge arises on the employee in respect of:
- (a) the value of the shares at the time of appropriation;
- (b) any increase in the value of the shares; or
- (c) any gain on the disposal of the shares (although capital gains tax is chargeable on any gain over the market value on appropriation).

Approved discretionary ('executive') share option schemes

Options held on 17 July 1995: (TA 1988 ss 185, 187, Sch 9)

Shares could be acquired at a discount of up to 15% of market value at the time of the grant where the employer also had an approved profit sharing scheme or an approved SAYE option scheme. No tax charge arose when the option was granted unless the price paid for the option plus the price at which the shares could be acquired was less than the market value of the shares, in which case, the discount was chargeable. In all other material respects, the rules are the same as for the CSOP schemes (see above).
The scheme was abolished for options granted after 16 July 1995.

Tax credits

From 6 April 2003, child tax credit ('CTC') and working tax credit ('WTC') replaced children's tax credit, working families' tax credit and disabled person's tax credit in addition to the child-related elements of certain other social security benefits. They are administered and paid by HMRC and are non-taxable. Claims must be made after the commencement of the tax year and can be backdated for a maximum of three months.

Child tax credit and working tax credit

	2008–09 Annual amount	2007–08 Annual amount
Child tax credit	£	£
Family element[1]	545	545
Addition for child under age of one[1]	545	545
Child element (for each child or young person)	2,085	1,845
Addition for disabled child or young person	2,540	2,440
Enhancement for severe disabled child or young person	1,020	980
Working tax credit	£	£
Basic element	1,800	1,730
Lone parent and couple element	1,770	1,700
30-hour element	735	705
Disability element	2,405	2,310
Severe disability element	1,020	980
50+ element – 16–29 hours worked	1,235	1,185
50+ element – 30 or more hours worked[2]	1,840	1,770
Childcare element (up to 80% (70% for 2005/06) of eligible costs)	Weekly	Weekly
– maximum eligible cost for one child	175	175
– maximum eligible cost for two or more children	300	300

[1]   Where an individual qualifies for the 50+ (30+ hours) payment, they cannot also qualify for the 50+ (16–29 hours) payment.

[2]   Only one family element available per family. The baby element is payable in addition in the first year of the child's life.

Income thresholds and withdrawal rates	2008–09	2007–08
First income threshold for those entitled to CTC and WTC	£6,420	£5,220
First withdrawal rate	39%	37%
Second income threshold	£50,000	£50,000
Second withdrawal rate	6.67%	6.67%
First threshold for those entitled to CTC only	£15,575	£14,495
Income disregarded	£25,000	£25,000

Calculation of award. Tax credits are awarded on an annual basis. They are initially based on the income of the claimant or joint claimants for the preceding tax year and then adjusted based on actual income in the tax year in which the credit is claimed.

Income broadly includes all taxable income excluding the first £300 of income from pensions, savings, property or foreign assets. If actual income is greater than the previous year's income by less than £25,000, the award is not adjusted. If actual income is less than the previous year's income or if it is greater than the previous year's income by £25,000 or more (£2,500 before April 2006), the award is adjusted to reflect actual income.

Where annual income exceeds the first income threshold, the excess is tapered (by 37%) and the balance deducted from the maximum tax credit entitlement. However, the family element of CTC is not reduced until income exceeds the second income threshold at which point the excess is tapered at 6.67%. The taper applies in order to the WTC elements, the WTC childcare elements, the CTC child elements and the CTC family elements.

Where circumstances change during a tax year and different rates apply, the award is recalculated on a proportional, daily basis. Such changes must be notified to HMRC within three months if tax credit entitlement will be reduced as a result. From April 2007, this time limit is reduced to one month.

Eligibility. CTC is payable to UK resident single parents and couples responsible for a child or young person. WTC is payable to UK residents who are at least 16 years old and who work (or in the case of a couple, one of whom works) at least 16 hours a week. Additionally, the claimant (or one of them if a couple) must either:

- be at least 25 years old and work at least 30 hours a week; or
- have a dependent child or children; or
- be over 50 and qualify for the 50+ element; or
- have a mental or physical disability which puts them at a disadvantage in getting a job and have previously been in receipt of some form of disability benefit.

Renewal claim. Claims for tax credit must be renewed by 31 July.

Inheritance tax

Rates of tax

From 15 March 1988 onwards

Cumulative gross transfer rate:	Rate
for gross transfers on death over the cumulative chargeable transfer limit	40%
for gross lifetime transfers over the cumulative chargeable transfer limit	20%
Grossing-up net transfer rate for each £1 over the chargeable transfer limit:	
for net transfers on death not bearing own tax	2/3
for net lifetime transfers	1/4

Cumulative chargeable transfer limits

Period	Limit	Period	Limit
	£		£
2010–11[1]	350,000	2000–01	234,000
2009–10[2]	325,000	1999–2000	231,000
2008–09[2]	**312,000**	1998–99	223,000
2007–08[3]	300,000	1997–98	215,000
2006–07	285,000	1996–97	200,000
2005–06	275,000	1995–96	154,000
2004–05	263,000	10.3.92–5.4.95	150,000
2003–04	255,000	6.4.91–9.3.92	140,000
2002–03	250,000	1990–91	128,000
2001–02	242,000	1989–90	118,000

[1]   FA 2007 s 4.
[2]   FA 2006 s 155.
[3]   FA 2005 s 98.

Any nil-rate band which is unused on a person's death can be transferred to their surviving spouse or civil partner for the purposes of the charge to tax on the death of the survivor on or after 9 October 2007.

Delivery of accounts: due dates

Type of transfer	Due date
Chargeable lifetime transfers	Later of: (a) 12 months after the end of the month in which the transfer took place; and (b) three months after the date on which the person delivering the account became liable
PETs which become chargeable	12 months after the end of the month in which the transferor died
Gifts with reservation chargeable on death	12 months after the end of the month in which the death occurred
Transfers on death	Later of: (a) 12 months after the end of the month in which the death occurred; and (b) three months after the date on which the personal representatives first act or the person liable first has reason to believe that he is liable to deliver an account
National heritage property	Six months after the end of the month in which the chargeable event occurred

Delivery of accounts: excepted transfers and estates

(SI 2002 No 1733, SI 2004 No 2543)

Date of transfer or death	6 April 2000–5 April 2002	6 April 2002–5 April 2003	6 April 2003–31 Aug 2006	From 1 Sept 2006
Excepted transfers:	*Value below*	*Value below*	*Value below*	*Value below*
Total chargeable transfers since 6 April	£10,000	£10,000	£10,000	£10,000
Total chargeable transfers during last ten years	£40,000	£40,000	£40,000	£40,000
Excepted estates:				
Total gross value	£210,000[1].	£220,000[1]	£240,000[1] (see (a) below)	(see (a) below)
Total gross value of property outside UK	£50,000	£75,000	£75,000	£100,000
Aggregate value of 'specified transfers'[2]	£75,000	£100,000	£100,000	£150,000
Settled property passing on death	–	£100,000	£100,000	£150,000

For chargeable transfers after 5 April 2007, no account need be delivered where:
(a)   the transfer is of cash or quoted shares or securities and the value of the transfer and other chargeable transfers made in the preceding seven years does not exceed the IHT threshold; or
(b)   the value of the transfer and other chargeable transfers made in the preceding seven years does not exceed 80% of the IHT threshold and the value of the transfer does not exceed the net amount of the threshold available to the transferor at the time of the transfer.

Excepted estates

For deaths occurring after 5 April 2004, no account need be delivered where the deceased died domiciled in the UK provided either conditions (a) or (b) below are met, and both conditions (c) and (d) below are met.
(a)   the aggregate of the gross value of the estate, and of any 'specified transfers' or 'specified exempt transfers'[3] does not exceed the appropriate IHT threshold;
(b)   the aggregate of the gross value of the estate, and of any 'specified transfers' or 'specified exempt transfers'[3] does not exceed £1,000,000; and after deducting from that aggregate figure any exempt spouse and charity transfers and total estate liabilities, it does not exceed the appropriate IHT threshold;
(c)   the gross value of settled property or foreign assets do not exceed the above limits; and
(d)   there were no chargeable lifetime transfers in the seven years before death other than specified transfers not exceeding the above limits.
For deaths occurring after 31 August 2006, an estate will not be an excepted estate if the provisions for alternatively secured pension funds in IHTA 1984 ss 151A–151C apply by reason of the individual's death.
For deaths after 5 April 2002 and before 6 April 2004, no account need be delivered where the deceased died domiciled in the UK provided that:
(vii)   the aggregate of the gross value of the estate, and of any 'specified transfers' does not exceed the above limits; and
(viii)   the gross value of settled property or foreign assets do not exceed the above limits; and
(ix)   there were no chargeable lifetime transfers in the seven years before death other than specified transfers not exceeding the above limits.
Where the deceased was never domiciled in the UK, no account need be delivered for deaths after 5 April 2002 provided that:
●   the value of the estate in the UK is wholly attributable to cash and quoted shares and securities not exceeding £150,000 (£100,000 before 1 September 2006); and
●   for deaths occurring after 31 August 2006, the provisions for alternatively secured pension funds in IHTA 1984 ss 151A–151C do not apply by reason of the individual's death.
[1]   This limit applies to the aggregate gross value of the estate and of 'specified transfers'[3].
[2]   'Specified transfers' are transfers of cash, quoted shares and securities and, after 6 April 2002, interests in or over land and, after 5 April 2004, personal chattels or corporeal moveable property.
[3]   'Specified exempt transfers' are transfers in the seven years before death between spouses, gifts to charity, political parties or housing associations, transfers to maintenance funds for historical buildings, etc or to employee trusts.

Excepted settlements

No account need be delivered of property comprised in excepted settlements where a chargeable event occurs after 5 April 2002. An 'excepted settlement' is one comprising solely of cash not exceeding £1,000 and in which there is no interest in possession. The trustees must be UK resident throughout the life of the trust and there must be no related settlements.

Reliefs

The following is a summary of the main reliefs and exemptions under the Inheritance Tax Act 1984. The legislation should be referred to for conditions and exceptions.

<table>
<tr><td colspan="4">Agricultural property</td></tr>
<tr><td colspan="2">Transfer with vacant possession (or right to obtain it within 12 months); transfer on or after 1 September 1995, of land let (or treated as let) on or after that date.</td><td colspan="2">100% of agricultural value</td></tr>
<tr><td colspan="2">Any other case</td><td colspan="2">50% of agricultural value</td></tr>
<tr><td colspan="4">Note: The 100% relief is extended in limited circumstances by Concession F17.</td></tr>
<tr><td colspan="3">Annual gifts</td><td>£3,000</td></tr>
<tr><td colspan="4">Business property</td></tr>
<tr><td>Unincorporated business</td><td>100%</td><td></td><td></td></tr>
<tr><td>Unquoted shares (including shares in AIM or USM companies) (held for 2 years or more)[1]</td><td>100%</td><td>Controlling holding in fully quoted companies</td><td>50%</td></tr>
<tr><td>Unquoted securities which alone, or together with other such securities and unquoted shares, give the transferor control of the company (held for 2 years or more)[1]</td><td>100%</td><td>Land, buildings, machinery or plant used in business of company or partnership</td><td>50%</td></tr>
<tr><td>Settled property used in life tenant's business</td><td>100%</td><td></td><td></td></tr>
</table>

[1] Tax charges arising and transfers occurring after 5 April 1996. 10 March 1992–5 April 1996 minority holding of shares or securities of up to 25% in unquoted or USM company qualified for 50% relief; larger holdings qualified for 100% relief.

<table>
<tr><td colspan="2">Charities, gifts to</td><td>Exempt</td></tr>
<tr><td colspan="3">From 1 April 2002, Community Amateur Sports Clubs are treated as charities</td></tr>
<tr><td colspan="3">Marriage gifts</td></tr>
<tr><td>Made by:</td><td>parent</td><td>£5,000</td></tr>
<tr><td></td><td>remoter ancestor</td><td>£2,500</td></tr>
<tr><td></td><td>party to marriage</td><td>£2,500</td></tr>
<tr><td></td><td>other person</td><td>£1,000</td></tr>
<tr><td colspan="3">National purposes</td></tr>
<tr><td colspan="2">Property given or bequeathed to bodies listed in IHTA 1984 Sch 3</td><td>Exempt</td></tr>
<tr><td colspan="2">Political parties, gifts to</td><td>Exempt</td></tr>
</table>

Potentially exempt transfers

Exempt if made 7 or more years before the date of death. Except for gifts with reservation etc, they include:

(a) transfers by individuals to other individuals or certain trusts for the disabled;

(b) transfers after 21 March 2006 by individuals to a bereaved minor's trust on the coming to an end of an immediate post-death interest;

(c) transfers before 22 March 2006 by individuals to accumulation and maintenance trusts;

(d) transfers by individuals into interest in possession trusts in which, for transfers after 21 March 2006, the beneficiary has a disabled person's interest; and

(e) certain transfers on the termination or disposal of an individual's beneficial interest in possession in settled property (in restricted circumstances following FA 2006).

Quick succession relief

Estate increased by chargeable transfer followed by death within 5 years

Death within 1st year	100%
Each additional year: decreased by	20%

Small gifts to same person £250

Spouses/civil partners with separate domicile (one not being in the UK)

Total exemption £55,000

Tapering relief

The value of the estate on death is taxed as the top slice of cumulative transfers in the 7 years before death. Transfers on or within 7 years of death are taxed on their value at the date of the gift on the death rate scale, but using the scale in force at the date of death, subject to the following taper:

Years between gift and death	Percentage of full charge at death rates
0–3	100
3–4	80
4–5	60
5–6	40
6–7	20

Penalties see p 12.

National insurance contributions

From 6 April 2008

Class 1 contributions[1]

Earnings limits and threshold		Weekly £	Monthly £	Yearly £
Lower earnings limit		90	390	4,680
Earnings threshold		105	453	5,435
Upper earnings limit		770	3,337	40,040

Not contracted out		Employees' contributions		Employers' contributions
Weekly earnings:	£105.01–£770	11%		12.8%
	Over £770	1%		12.8%

Contracted out			Salary-related schemes	Money purchase schemes
Weekly earnings:	£105.01–£770	9.4%	9.1%	11.4%
	Over £770	1%	12.8%	12.8%
	– rebate £90–£105	1.6%[2]	3.7%	1.4%

Women at reduced rate				
Weekly earnings:	£105.01–£770	4.85%	*as above*	
	Over £770	1%	*as above*	

Class 1A and Class 1B contributions	12.8%

[1] Employees' rates are nil for children under 16, men over 65 and women over 60 but employers' contributions are still payable. NICs are not payable on earnings up to the earnings threshold.

[2] The rebate is given on earnings between the lower earnings limit and the earnings threshold. The rebate for employees is given to employers to the extent that insufficient contributions have been paid by the employee for offset.

6 April 2007–5 April 2008

Class 1 contributions[1]

Earnings limits and threshold		Weekly £	Monthly £	Yearly £
Lower earnings limit		87	377	4,524
Earnings threshold		100	435	5,225
Upper earnings limit		670	2,904	34,840

Not contracted out		Employees' contributions		Employers' contributions
Weekly earnings:	£100.01–£670	11%		12.8%
	Over £670	1%		12.8%

Contracted out			Salary-related schemes	Money purchase schemes
Weekly earnings:	£100.01–£670	9.4%	9.1%	11.4%
	Over £670	1%	12.8%	12.8%
	– rebate £87–£100	1.6%[2]	3.7%	1.4%

Women at reduced rate				
Weekly earnings:	£100.01–£670	4.85%	*as above*	
	Over £670	1%	*as above*	

Class 1A and Class 1B contributions	12.8%

[1] Employees' rates are nil for children under 16, men over 65 and women over 60 but employers' contributions are still payable. NICs are not payable on earnings up to the earnings threshold.

[2] The rebate is given on earnings between the lower earnings limit and the earnings threshold. The rebate for employees is given to employers to the extent that insufficient contributions have been paid by the employee for offset.

6 April 2006–5 April 2007

Class 1 contributions[1]				
Earnings limits and threshold		Weekly £	Monthly £	Yearly £
Lower earnings limit		84	364	4,368
Earnings threshold		97	420	5,035
Upper earnings limit		645	2,795	33,540
Not contracted out		**Employees' contributions**		**Employers' contributions**
Weekly earnings:	£97.01–£645	11%		12.8%
	Over £645	1%		12.8%
Contracted out			*Salary-related schemes*	*Money purchase schemes*
Weekly earnings:	£97.01–£645	9.4%	9.3%	11.4%
	Over £645	1%	12.8%	12.8%
	– rebate £84–£97	1.6%[2]	3.5%	1%
Women at reduced rate				
Weekly earnings:	£97.01–£645	4.85%	*as above*	
	Over £645	1%	*as above*	
Class 1A and Class 1B contributions				12.8%

[1] Employees' rates are nil for children under 16, men over 65 and women over 60 but employers' contributions are still payable. NICs are not payable on earnings up to the earnings threshold.

[2] The rebate is given on earnings between the lower earnings limit and the earnings threshold. The rebate for employees is given to employers to the extent that insufficient contributions have been paid by the employee for offset.

6 April 2005–5 April 2006

Class 1 contributions[1]				
Earnings limits and threshold		Weekly £	Monthly £	Yearly £
Lower earnings limit		82	356	4,264
Earnings threshold		94	408	4,895
Upper earnings limit		630	2,730	32,760
Not contracted out		**Employees' contributions**		**Employers' contributions**
Weekly earnings:	£94.01–£630	11%		12.8%
	Over £630	1%		12.8%
Contracted out			*Salary-related schemes*	*Money purchase schemes*
Weekly earnings:	£94.01–£630	9.4%	9.3%	11.8%
	Over £630	1%	12.8%	12.8%
	– rebate £82–£94	1.6%[2]	3.5%	1%
Women at reduced rate				
Weekly earnings:	£94.01–£630	4.85%	*as above*	
	Over £630	1%	*as above*	
Class 1A and Class 1B contributions				12.8%

[1] Employees' rates are nil for children under 16, men over 65 and women over 60 but employers' contributions are still payable. NICs are not payable on earnings up to the earnings threshold.

[2] The rebate is given on earnings between the lower earnings limit and the earnings threshold. The rebate for employees is given to employers to the extent that insufficient contributions have been paid by the employee for offset.

6 April 2004–5 April 2005

Class 1 contributions[1]

Earnings limits and threshold		Weekly £	Monthly £	Yearly £
Lower earnings limit		79	343	4,108
Earnings threshold		91	395	4,745
Upper earnings limit		610	2,644	31,720

Not contracted out		**Employees' contributions**		**Employers' contributions**
Weekly earnings:	£91.01–£610	11%		12.8%
	Over £610	1%		12.8%

Contracted out			*Salary-related schemes*	*Money purchase schemes*
Weekly earnings:	£91.01–£610	9.4%	9.3%	11.8%
	Over £610	1%	12.8%	12.8%
	– rebate £79–£91	1.6%[2]	3.5%	1%

Women at reduced rate				
Weekly earnings:	£91.01–£610	4.85%	*as above*	
	Over £610	1%	*as above*	

Class 1A and Class 1B contributions	12.8%

[1] Employees' rates are nil for children under 16, men over 65 and women over 60 but employers' contributions are still payable. NICs are not payable on earnings up to the earnings threshold.

[2] The rebate is given on earnings between the lower earnings limit and the earnings threshold. The rebate for employees is given to employers to the extent that insufficient contributions have been paid by the employee for offset.

6 April 2003–5 April 2004

Class 1 contributions[1]

Earnings limits and threshold		Weekly £	Monthly £	Yearly £
Lower earnings limit		77	334	4,004
Earnings threshold		89	385	4,615
Upper earnings limit		595	2,579	30,940

Not contracted out		**Employees' contributions**		**Employers' contributions**
Weekly earnings:	£89.01–£595	11%		12.8%
	Over £595	1%		12.8%

Contracted out			*Salary-related schemes*	*Money purchase schemes*
Weekly earnings:	£89.01–£595	9.4%	9.3%	11.8%
	Over £595	1%	12.8%	12.8%
	– rebate £77–£89	1.6%[2]	3.5%	1%

Women at reduced rate				
Weekly earnings:	£89.01–£595	4.85%	*as above*	
	Over £595	1%	*as above*	

Class 1A and Class 1B contributions	12.8%

[1] Employees' rates are nil for children under 16, men over 65 and women over 60 but employers' contributions are still payable. NICs are not payable on earnings up to the earnings threshold.

[2] The rebate is given on earnings between the lower earnings limit and the earnings threshold. The rebate for employees is given to employers to the extent that insufficient contributions have been paid by the employee for offset.

Class 2, 3 and 4 contributions

	2008–09	2007–08	2006–07
Class 2 (self-employed)			
Flat rate—per week	2.30	£2.20	£2.10
Share fishermen—per week	2.95	£2.85	£2.75
Volunteer development workers—per week	4.50	£4.35	£4.20
Small earning exception—per year	4,825	£4,635	£4,465
Class 3 (voluntary contributions)			
Flat rate—per week	8.10	£7.80	£7.55
Class 4 (self-employed)[1]			
Lower annual profits limit	5,435	£5,225	£5,035
Upper annual profits limit	40,040	£34,840	£33,540
Rate between lower and upper limits	8%	8%	8%
Rate on profits above upper limit	1%	1%	1%
Maximum contributions			
Class 1 or Class 1/Class 2[2]	3,876.95	£3,323.10	£3,194.84
– plus rate on earnings above upper limit	1%	1%	1%
Class 4 limiting amount[3]	2,890.30	£2,485.80	£2,391.70
– plus rate on profits above upper limit	1%	1%	1%

[1] Not payable if pensionable age is reached by the beginning of the tax year.

[2] Where an earner has more than one employment (including self-employment), liability for Class 1 or Class 1 and Class 2 contributions cannot exceed a maximum amount equal to 53 employees' Class 1 contributions at the maximum standard rate, plus, from 2003–04 onwards, 1% on earnings over the individual's upper earnings limit (which varies depending on individual circumstances).

[3] Where Class 4 contributions are payable in addition to Class 1 and/or Class 2 contributions, liability for Class 4 contributions cannot exceed such an amount as, when added to the Class 1/Class 2 contributions payable (after applying the maximum if appropriate), equals the limiting amount. The limiting amount is the maximum Class 4 contributions payable (including, from 2003–04 onwards, 1% on earnings over the upper profit limit) plus 53 Class 2 contributions.

	2005–06	2004–05	2003–04
Class 2 (self-employed)			
Flat rate—per week	£2.10	£2.05	£2.00
Share fishermen—per week	£2.75	£2.70	£2.65
Volunteer development workers—per week	£4.10	£3.95	£3.85
Small earning exception—per year	£4,345	£4,215	£4,095
Class 3 (voluntary contributions)			
Flat rate—per week	£7.35	£7.15	£6.95
Class 4 (self-employed)[1]			
Lower annual profits limit	£4,895	£4,745	£4,615
Upper annual profits limit	£32,760	£31,720	£30,940
Rate between lower and upper limits	8%	8%	8%
Rate on profits above upper limit	1%	1%	1%
Maximum contributions			
Class 1 or Class 1/Class 2[2]	£3,124.88	£3,205.77	£2,949.98
– plus rate on earnings above upper limit	1%	1%	1%
Class 4 limiting amount[3]	£2,340.50	£2,266.65	£2,212.00
– plus rate on profits above upper limit	1%	1%	1%

[1] Not payable if pensionable age is reached by the beginning of the tax year.

[2] Where an earner has more than one employment (including self-employment), liability for Class 1 or Class 1 and Class 2 contributions cannot exceed a maximum amount equal to 53 employees' Class 1 contributions at the maximum standard rate, plus, from 2003–04 onwards, 1% on earnings over the individual's upper earnings limit (which varies depending on individual circumstances).

[3] Where Class 4 contributions are payable in addition to Class 1 and/or Class 2 contributions, liability for Class 4 contributions cannot exceed such an amount as, when added to the Class 1/Class 2 contributions payable (after applying the maximum if appropriate), equals the limiting amount. The limiting amount is the maximum Class 4 contributions payable (including, from 2003–04 onwards, 1% on earnings over the upper profit limit) plus 53 Class 2 contributions.

Employers' contributions: benefits in kind

Class 1A national insurance contributions are payable by employers on most taxable benefits in kind, excluding benefits:
(1) which are covered by a dispensation;
(2) included in a PAYE settlement agreement;
(3) provided to employees not earning more than £8,500 pa (including benefits in kind and expenses payments);
(4) otherwise not required to be included on a P11D;
(5) on which Class 1 national insurance contributions were due.

Class 1B contributions are payable by employers by reference to the value of any items included in a PAYE settlement agreement (PSA) which would otherwise be earnings for Class 1 or Class 1A, including the amount of tax paid. Income tax and Class 1B contributions on a PSA are payable by 19 October after the end of the tax year to which the PSA relates.

Common benefits subject to Class 1 and Class 1A NICs (CWG5 2006)

Benefit	NICs Class	PAYE or P11D
Assets/gifts given to employees*	1A	P11D
Assets loaned to employees	1A	P11D
Car or van fuel supplied for private motoring	1A	P11D
Cars or vans available for private use	1A	P11D
Car parking other than at or near place of work or as part of business travel*	1A	P11D
Christmas gifts – cash	1	PAYE
– benefits	1A	P11D
Clothing and uniforms		
– cash payment for clothing that can be worn at any time	1	PAYE
– cash payment for clothing that can only be worn at work or non-durable items such as tights or stockings	–	PAYE
– clothing provided by employer that can be worn at any time	1A	P11D
Computers provided for private use where value exceeds £2,500 (all computers provided for private use after 5.4.06)	1A	P11D
Credit cards and tokens – personal expenses not reimbursed	1	P11D
Entertaining – non-business staff expenses/allowances*	1A	P11D
Holidays provided*	1A	P11D
Living accommodation (beneficial)	1A	P11D
Loans – at low interest or interest-free	1A	P11D
– written off	1	P11D
Meals provided other than at canteen or at business premises open to all staff on a reasonable scale	1A	P11D
Medical insurance or treatment provided in the UK by employer	1A	P11D
Notional payments	1	PAYE
Payments in kind convertible to cash	1	PAYE
Payments of employees' personal liabilities	1	PAYE
Prize money	1	PAYE
Relocation payments – qualifying over £8,000	1A	P11D
– non-qualifying benefits	1A	P11D
– non-qualifying expenses	1	P11D
Round sum allowances (not identified as business expense)	1	PAYE
Scholarships awarded to students because of parent's employment or payment of school fees*	1A	P11D
Services supplied	1A	P11D
Tax paid for and not reimbursed by employee	1	P11D
Telephone rental and private calls – employer subscribes*	1A	P11D
Vouchers (other than exceptions for childcare, meals, etc)	1	P11D

* Reimbursement of or payment for goods or services for personal use by employee or payment of personal expenses or allowances where the employee contracts with the supplier is subject to Class 1 NICs and is reportable on form P11D.

Overseas

Average rates of exchange

Average for year ending	31.3.06	31.12.06	31.03.07	31.12.07	31.03.08
Algeria (Dinar)	130.3635	134.0142	136.9221	139.34	137.08
Argentina (Peso)	5.2768	5.652	5.8223	6.2363	6.283
Australia ($A)	2.37825	2.4448	2.4739	2.3907	2.3153
Bahrain (Dinar)	0.6729	0.6952	0.7141	0.754	0.7562
Bangladesh (Taka)	117.237	127.3866	131.2303	138.02	138.23
Barbados (BD$)	3.57	3.6879	3.7884	4.0023	4.0151
Bolivia (Boliviano)	14.36	14.7464	15.1462	15.7073	15.5431
Botswana (Pula)	9.51	10.8192	11.4887	12.2795	12.4328
Brazil (Real)	4.1126	4.0028	4.0789	3.8951	3.7214
Brunei ($)	2.9546	2.9251	2.9649	3.0127	2.9581
Bulgaria (Lev)				2.8506	2.7593
Burma (Kyat)	11.4616	11.8406	12.1615	12.8474	12.8986
Burundi (Franc)	1,839.63	1,846.6517	1,932.3958	2,180.06	2,246.85
Canada (Can$)	2.1598	2.0901	2.1567	2.1484	2.0725
Cayman Islands (CI$)	1.4774	1.5712	1.6242	1.7029	1.6912
Chile (Peso)	975.9229	977.173	1,010.6452	1,043.21	1,007.89
China (Renminbi Yuan)	14.4759	14.7126	14.9935	15.2109	14.944
Colombia (Peso)	4,107.4241	4,348.138	4441.0926	4,150.21	4,009.40
Congo Dem Rep (Zaire) (Congolese Franc)	864.3402	859.2795	935.6975	1,111.48	1,116.84
Costa Rica (Colon)	869.708	946.8613	981.3863	1,033.37	1,025.41
Cuba (Peso)	1.7815	1.8483	1.901	1.9787	1.9719
Cyprus (£)	0.8417	0.8434	0.8508	0.8494	0.84398
1.4.07 to 21.12.07					0.84398
Euro from 1.1.08					
Czech Republic (Koruna)	43.1314	41.4016	41.5989	40.4435	38.2403
Denmark (Krone)	10.93255	10.9397	11.0014	10.8900	10.5702
Egypt (£)	10.2955	10.5864	10.8563	11.2921	11.226
El Salvador (Colon)	15.5912	16.1758	16.6369	17.5503	17.6071
Ethiopia (Birr)	15.5295	16.1638	16.7003	18.0963	18.4057
European Union (Euro)	1.4664	1.4666	1.475	1.4604	1.4178
Fiji Islands (F$)	3.0556	3.2042	3.2532	3.2178	3.1500
French Cty/Africa (CFA franc)	961.102	960.8382	967.3428	956.12	925.47
French Pacific Is (CFP franc)	174.724	174.6763	175.8587	173.82	168.25
Gambia (Dalasi)	50.3634	51.8573	53.0478	49.573	46.5553
Ghana (Cedi)	16,225.61	16,916.4967	17,447.0667	16,916.4967	17,447.0667
1.1.07 to 30.6.07				18,264.02	
1.7.07 to 31.12.07				1.927	
1.4.07 to 30.6.07					18,434.15
1.7.07 to 31.3.08					1.9257
Grenada/Wind. Isles (EC$)	4.8195	4.9787	5.1144	5.4032	5.4204
Guyana (G$)	334.5235	350.4058	365.1609	406.10	409.02
Honduras (Lempira)	33.6188	34.9226	35.9179	37.8929	38.016
Hong Kong (HK$)	13.9682	14.3132	14.724	15.6114	15.659
Hungary (Forint)	367.705	386.9914	388.1129	366.12	356.86
Iceland (Krona)	113.7708	128.9847	133.7177	127.99	128.36
India (Rupee)	78.8637	83.4523	85.6028	82.6063	80.7528
Indonesia (Rupiah)	17,323.1629	16,875.1042	17,253.2658	18,294.55	18,425.14
Iran (Rial)	16,111.9	16,908.4704	17,424.415	18,566.81	18,630.05
Iraq (Dinar)	2,620.743	2,699.6693	2,685.7928	2,510.79	2,479.81
Israel (Shekel)	8.1412	8.2066	8.2179	8.2105	7.9471
Jamaica (J$)	112.3691	121.3518	125.8431	138.11	140.35
Japan (Yen)	201.2374	214.3005	221.4527	235.6273	229.3116
Jordan (Dinar)	1.2648	1.3066	1,3422	1.4178	1.4222
Kenya (Shilling)	132.8881	132.9039	135.298	134.68	134.00
Korea South (Won)	1,797.1	1,757.86	1,794.2808	1,861.77	1,877.73

Average for year ending	31.3.06	31.12.06	31.03.07	31.12.07	31.03.08
Kuwait (Dinar)	0.5213	0.535	0.5483	0.5687	0.5618
Laos (New Kip)	18,440.6	18,530.2392	18,804.8133	19,225.02	18,955.83
Latvia (lats)				1.0206	0.9855
Lebanon (£)	2,687.5416	2,780.1683	2,859.8993	3,026.21	3,035.80
Libya (Dinar)	2.3642	2.4064	2.4467	2.519	2.4937
Lithuania (Litas)				5.0329	4.8715
Malawi (Kwacha)	220.5461	251.0676	262.3102	280.16	281.54
Malaysia (Ringgit)	6.7233	6.7564	6.832	6.8706	6.7553
Malta (Lira)	0.6293	0.63	0.6338		
Up to 31.12.07				0.6271	
1.4.07 to 31.12.07					0.62236
Euro from 1.1.08					
Mauritius (Rupee)	53.3423	57.9506	60.4041	62.0963	59.8987
Mexico (Peso)	19.1852	20.0984	20.8418	21.8598	21.8287
Morocco (Dirham)	16.0777	16.186	16.3655	16.3605	15.9354
Nepal (Rupee)	125.954	133.8618	137.3187	132.02	129.13
N'nd Antilles (Guilder)	3.1888	3.3084	3.4027	3.5895	3.6011
New Zealand(NZ$)	2.5841	2.8425	2.8853	2.7195	2.6436
Nicaragua (Gold Cordoba)	29.6126	32.1564	33.5507	37.0597	37.6291
Nigeria (Naira)	235.493	236.971	242.9804	251.46	246.92
Norway (Krone)	11.6878	11.8095	11.9303	11.7296	11.3122
Oman (Rial Omani)	0.6873	0.7099	0.7293	0.7702	0.7726
Pakistan (Rupee)	106.6047	111.1701	114.5979	121.51	122.81
Papua New Guinea (Kina)	5.4038	5.5053	5.6454	5.8123	5.7172
Paraguay (Guarani)	10,913.66	10,373.1821	10,251.0069	10,055.95	9,823.32
Peru (New Sol)	5.9161	6.0317	6.1252	6.2554	6.1231
Philippines (Peso)	96.8521	94.5009	95.5121	92.1586	88.695
Poland (Zloty)	5.8289	5.7126	5.7668	5.4989	5.2082
Portugal (Euro)	1.4664				
Qatar (Riyal)	6.4968	6.7125	6.8958	7.2833	7.3053
Romania (Leu)		5.1527	5.1239	4.8646	4.8313
1.07.05 to 31.03.06	5.2306				
Russia (Rouble-Market)	50.4621	50.0151	50.6508	51.1028	50.1627
Rwanda (R Franc)	967.81	1,010.6548	1,042.4532	1,096.84	1,098.52
Saudi Arabia (Riyal)	6.6944	6.9151	7.1037	7.4983	7.5217
Seychelles (Rupee)	9.8347	10.2716	10.8403	13.6354	14.6353
Sierra Leone (Leone)	5,130.52	5,461.5218	5,631.4166	5,972.91	5,987.38
Singapore (S$)	2.9663	2.9308	2.966	3.0131	2.9616
Slovakia (Koruna)				49.234	47.1771
Solomon Islands (SI$)	13.1391	13.597	13.9149	14.509	14.6865
Somali Republic (Schilling)	3,841.33	2,615.015	2,599.6275	2,745.39	2,270.69
South Africa (Rand)	11.4532	12.4976	13.341	14.1085	14.3067
Sri Lanka (Rupee)	180.6214	191.8051	200.1501	221.39	221.61
Sudan (Dinar to 30.6.07, £ thereafter)	424.337	399.0983	397.5664		397.5664
1.1.07 to 30.6.07				397.24	
1.7.07 to 31.12.07				4.1168	
1.4.07 to 30.6.07					400.6417
1.7.07 to 31.3.08					4.0913
Surinam (Dollar)	4.8734	5.0713	5.218	5.5045	5.5224
Swaziland (Lilangeli)	11.4034	12.6018	13.4435	14.0461	14.3204
Sweden (Krona)	13.67855	13.5672	13.593	13.5236	13.1967
Switzerland (Franc)	2.2756	2.3074	2.3425	2.4010	2.3261
Syria (Pound)	93.0719	96.5596	99.2471	103.71	103.50
Taiwan (New T$)	57.7011	59.9643	61.8966	65.7326	65.258
Tanzania (Schilling)	2,052.1933	2,311.7583	2,411.6028	2,481.21	2,437.04
Thailand (Baht)	72.1171	69.7902	69.3549	68.5207	67.7565
Tonga Islands (Pa'Anga)	3.2585	3.7453	3.8224	3.908	3.8389
Trinidad and Tobago (TT$)	11.1882	11.58	11.9098	12.6152	12.6561
Tunisia (Dinar)	2.3656	2.4507	2.4998	2.5590	2.5108

Average rates of exchange – continued

Average for year ending	31.3.06	31.12.06	31.03.07	31.12.07	31.03.08
Turkey (Lira)		2.6492	2.7546	2.6067	2.5166
1.1.05 to 31.3.05	2.4068				
Uganda (New Shilling)	3,221.231	3,375.2477	3,440.7299	3,451.92	3,429.98
United Arab Emirates (Dirham)	6.5562	6.7727	6.9571	7.3481	7.3712
Uruguay (Peso Uruguayo)	43.1552	44.2834	45.5669	46.9076	45.3662
USA (US$)	1.79738	1.8424	1.8932	2.0020	2.0080
Venezuela (Bolivar to 31.12.07, Bolivar Fuerte thereafter)	4,751.6019	5,044.842	5,747.9573	5,357.25	
1.4.07 to 31.12.07					4,665.73
1.1.08 to 31.3.08					4.2501
Vietnam (Dong)	28,298.4	29,567.2417	30,455.15	32,241.04	32,340.43
Yemen (Rial)	345.207	364.4703	376.1672	398.84	400.27
Zambia (Kwacha)	7,310.1153	6,622.279	7,244.9871	7,984.03	7,769.02
Zimbabwe (Dollar)					
22.10.05 to 31.3.06	144,586.50				
1.1.06 to 3.8.06		178,951.06			
4.8.06 to 31.12.06		476.63			
1.4.06 to 3.8.06			185,137.83		
4.8.06 to 31.3.07			481.06		
1.1.07 to 5.9.07				496.04	
6.9.07 to 31.12.07				61,053.83	
1.4.07 to 5.9.07					500.60
6.9.07 to 31.3.08					60,335.72

Rates of exchange on year-end dates

	31.3.06	29.12.06	30.03.07	31.12.07	31.03.08
Australia ($A)	2.4326	2.4779	2.4279	2.2671	2.1773
Canada (Can$)	2.0235	2.2776	2.2627	1.9646	2.0393
Denmark (Krone)	10.6962	11.0641	10.9789	10.1522	9.3536
European Union (Euro)	1.4333	1.4842	1.4735	1.3615	1.2543
Hong Kong (HK$)	13.4598	15.2213	15.3265	15.5215	15.4685
Japan (Yen)	204.660	233.204	231.586	222.380	197.826
Norway (Krone)	11.3835	12.1859	11.9723	10.8087	10.1000
South Africa (Rand)	10.6926	13.7994	14.2247	13.6045	16.1515
Sweden (Krona)	13.5185	13.3928	13.7611	12.8656	11.7858
Switzerland (Franc)	2.2668	2.3891	2.3945	2.2536	1.9658
USA (US$)	1.7346	1.9572	1.9614	1.9906	1.9875

Note: The material on p 80–82 is reproduced from information provided by HMRC and is Crown copyright.

Double taxation agreements (including protocols and regulations)

Agreements in force covering taxes on income and capital gains

Country	SI/SR & O	Country	SI/SR & O
Antigua & Barbuda	**1947/2865**	Greece	**1954/142**
	1968/1096	Grenada	**1949/361**
Argentina	**1997/1777**		1968/1867
Armenia[1]		Guernsey	**1952/1215**
Australia	**2003/3199**		1994/3209
Austria	**1970/1947**	Guyana	**1992/3207**
	1979/117	Hungary	**1978/1056**
	1994/768	Iceland	**1991/2879**
Azerbaijan	**1995/762**	India	**1993/1801**
Bangladesh	**1980/708**	Indonesia	**1994/769**
Barbados	**1970/952**	Irish Republic	**1976/2151**
	1973/2096		1976/2152
Belarus[1]	**1986/224**		1995/764
Belgium	**1987/2053**		1998/3151
Belize	**1947/2866**	Isle of Man	**1955/1205**
	1968/573		1991/2880
	1973/2097		1994/3208
Bolivia	**1995/2707**	Israel	**1963/616**
Bosnia Herzegovina[2]	**1981/1815**		1971/391
Botswana	**2006/1925**	Italy	**1990/2590**
Brunei	**1950/1977**	Ivory Coast	**1987/169**
	1968/306	Jamaica	**1973/1329**
	1973/2098	Japan	**2006/1924**
Bulgaria	**1987/2054**	Jersey	**1952/1216**
Canada	**1980/709**		1994/3210
	1980/1528	Jordan	**2001/3924**
	1985/1996	Kazakhstan	**1994/3211**
	2003/2619		1998/2567
Chile	**2003/3200**	Kenya	**1977/1299**
China[4]	**1984/1826**	Kiribati (and Tuvalu)	**1950/750**
	1996/3164		1968/309
Croatia[2]	**1981/1815**		1974/1271
Cyprus	**1975/425**	Korea (South)	**1996/3168**
	1980/1529	Kuwait	**1999/2036**
Czech Republic[3]	**1991/2876**	Kyrgyzstan[1]	
Denmark	**1980/1960**	Latvia	**1996/3167**
	1991/2877	Lesotho	**1997/2986**
	1996/3165	Lithuania[1]	**2001/3925**
Egypt	**1980/1091**		2002/2847
Estonia	**1994/3207**	Luxembourg	**1968/1100**
Falkland Islands	**1997/2985**		1980/567
Faroes	**2007/3469**		1984/364
Fiji	**1976/1342**	Macedonia[2]	**2007/2127**
Finland	**1970/153**	Malawi	**1956/619**
	1980/710		1964/1401
	1985/1997		1968/1101
	1991/2878		1979/302
	1996/3166	Malaysia	**1997/2987**
France	**1968/1869**	Malta	**1995/763**
	1973/1328	Mauritius	**1981/1121**
	1987/466		1987/467
	1987/2055		2003/2620
Gambia	**1980/1963**	Mexico	**1994/3212**
Georgia[1]	**2004/3325**	Moldova[1]	2008/1795
Germany	**1967/25**	Mongolia	**1996/2598**
	1971/874	Montenegro[2]	**1981/1815**
Ghana	**1993/1800**	Montserrat	**1947/2869**

Country	SI/SR & O	Country	SI/SR & O
	1968/576		1968/574
Morocco	**1991/2881**		1974/1270
Myanmar (Burma)	**1952/751**	South Africa	**2002/3138**
Namibia	**1962/2352**	Spain	1976/1919
	1967/1490		1995/765
Netherlands	**1980/1961**	Sri Lanka	**1980/713**
	1990/2152	Sudan	**1977/1719**
New Zealand	**1984/365**	Swaziland	**1969/380**
	2004/1274	Sweden	**1984/366**
	2008/1793	Switzerland	**2007/3465**
Nigeria	**1987/2057**	Taiwan	**2002/3137**
Norway	**2000/3247**	Tajikistan[1]	**1986/224**
Oman	**1998/2568**	Thailand	**1981/1546**
Pakistan	**1987/2058**	Trinidad and Tobago	**1983/1903**
Papua New Guinea	**1991/2882**	Tunisia	**1984/133**
Philippines	**1978/184**	Turkey	**1988/932**
Poland	**2006/3323**	Turkmenistan[1]	**1986/224**
Portugal	**1969/599**	Tuvalu (and Kiribati)	**1950/750**
Romania	**1977/57**		1968/309
Russian Federation	**1994/3213**		1974/1271
St Kitts and Nevis	**1947/2872**	Uganda	**1993/1802**
Saudi Arabia	2008/1770	Ukraine	**1993/1803**
Serbia[2]	**1981/1815**	USA	**2002/2848**
Sierra Leone	**1947/2873**	Uzbekistan	**1994/770**
	1968/1104	Venezuela	**1996/2599**
Singapore	**1997/2988**	Vietnam	**1994/3216**
Slovak Republic[3]	**1991/2876**	Zambia	**1972/1721**
Slovenia[2]	**2008/1796**		1981/1816
Solomon Islands	**1950/748**	Zimbabwe	**1982/1842**

[1] Following the dissolution of the USSR, new agreements have come into force with Azerbaijan, Estonia, Kazakhstan, Latvia, Lithuania, Moldova the Russian Federation, Ukraine and Uzbekistan. *SI 1986 No 224* (the former USSR agreement) is treated as continuing to apply to Belarus, Tajikistan and Turkmenistan (in the case of Belarus until the coming into force of *SI 1995 No 2706*). It was similarly so treated by the UK until 31 March 2002 in the case of Armenia, Georgia, Kyrgyzstan and Lithuania (none of which considered itself bound by that convention) but as ceasing so to apply after that date (although new treaties are in force with Lithuania and Georgia). (SP 4/01).

[2] *SI 1981 No 1815* (the former Yugoslavia agreement) is treated as remaining in force between the UK and, respectively, Bosnia-Herzegovina, Croatia and Serbia and Montenegro. (SP 3/2004). Negotiations for a new double taxation convention are taking place with Croatia, Serbia and Montenegro and Slovenia (Revenue Press Release, 29 September 2004).

[3] *SI 1991 No 2876* (the former Czechoslovakia agreement) is treated as remaining in force between the UK and, respectively, the Czech Republic and the Slovak Republic. (SP 5/93).

[4] *SI 1984 No 1826* does not apply to the Hong Kong Special Administrative Region.

Agreements in force covering shipping and air transport profits

Country	SI/SR & O	Country	SI/SR & O
Algeria (air)	1984/362	Iran (air)	1960/2419
Armenia (USSR air)*	1974/1269		
Belarus (USSR air)*	1974/1269	Kyrgyzstan (USSR air)*	1974/1269
Brazil	1968/572	Lebanon	1964/278
Cameroon (air)	1982/1841	Moldova (USSR air)*	1974/1269
China (air)	1981/1119	Saudi Arabia (air)	1994/767
Congo Democratic Republic	1977/1298	Tajikistan (USSR air)*	1974/1269
Ethiopia (air)	1977/1297	Turkmenistan (USSR air)*	1974/1269
Georgia (USSR air)*	1974/1269		
Hong Kong (air)	1998/2566		
(shipping)	2000/3248		

* HMRC have confirmed that this Arrangement will be treated in the same way as the Convention covering income and capital gains (SI 1986/224). See note 1 on page 84.

Agreements in force covering estates, inheritances and gifts

France*	1963/1319	Pakistan*	1957/1522
India*	1956/998	South Africa	1979/576
Ireland	1978/1107	Sweden	1981/840
Italy*	1968/304		1989/986
Netherlands	1980/706	Switzerland	1994/3214
	1996/730	USA	1979/1454

* Agreements pre-date UK inheritance tax/capital transfer tax.

Overseas income – basis of assessment

	Professions, trades, etc	Pensions	Other income
Non-residents	Exempt	Exempt	Exempt
Residents			
(1) Foreign domicile	Remittance	Remittance	Remittance
(2) UK domicile			
(a) Non Commonwealth citizen[1]	Arising	90%[3] arising	Arising
(b) Commonwealth citizen[2]			
(i) ordinarily resident	Arising	90%[4] arising	Arising
(ii) not ordinarily resident	Remittance	Remittance	Remittance

[1] But not citizen of the Republic of Ireland.

[2] Or citizen of the Republic of Ireland.

[3] Pensions paid by the governments of the Federal Republic of Germany or of Austria to victims of Nazi persecution are exempt.

[4] Where from 6 April 2008, an individual with a domicile outside the UK who has overseas income or gains in excess of £2,000 claims the remittance basis, he will not qualify for personal allowances or the capital gains tax annual exemption. The claim for remittance basis must be made annually. If the individual is not UK domiciled or ordinarily resident in a year and has been resident in the UK for seven out of the last nine years and has overseas income or gains in excess of £2,000, there is an additional charge of 30,000.

Employment income liability of non-resident employees see p 59.

Tax-free (FOTRA) securities

Interest on all government stock is exempt from tax where the beneficial owner is not ordinarily resident in the UK (FA 1996 s 154; FA 1998 s 161; ITTOIA 2005 ss 713, 714). Except in the case of 31/2% War Loan 1952 or after, the exemption does not apply where the securities are held for the purposes of a trade or business carried on in the UK.

Social security benefits

Taxable state benefits

	Weekly 7.4.08	Total 2008/09 (52 weeks)	Weekly 9.4.07 onwards	Total 2007/08 (52 weeks)
	£	£	£	£
Bereavement benefits[1]				
Standard rate (widow's pension)	90.70	4,716	87.30	4,540
Widowed parent's allowance	90.70	4,716	87.30	4,540
Carer's allowance	50.55	2,628	48.65	2,530
– Adult dependency increase	30.20	1,570	29.05	1,511
Incapacity benefit				
Long-term (after 52 weeks)	84.50	4,394	81.35	4,230
– Adult dependency increase	50.55	2,628	48.65	2,530
– Age increase: higher rate	17.75	923	17.10	889
lower rate	8.90	462	8.55	445
Short term[2]				
– Under pension age: higher rate	75.40	–	72.55	–
– Adult dependency increase	39.40	–	37.90	–
– Over pension age: higher rate	84.50	–	81.35	–
– Adult dependency increase	48.65	–	46.80	–
Industrial death benefit[3]				
Widow's pension: higher rate	90.70	4,716	87.30	4,540
lower rate	27.21	1,414	26.19	1,362
Widower's pension	90.70	4,716	87.30	4,540
Invalidity allowance[4]				
Higher rate	17.75	923	17.10	889
Middle rate	11.40	592	11.00	572
Lower rate	5.70	296	5.50	286
Jobseeker's allowance[5]				
Single: under 18	47.95	–	35.65	–
18–24	47.95	–	46.85	–
25 or over	60.50	–	59.15	–
State pension				
Single person (Category A or B)	90.70	4,716	87.30	4,540
Couple – if both contributors	181.40	9,432	174.60	9,079
– if wife non-contributor	145.05	7,542	139.60	7,259
Adult dependency increase	54.35	2,826	52.30	2,720
Non-contributory pension				
– single (Category C or D)	54.35	2,826	52.30	2,720
– couple (Category C)	86.85	4,516	83.60	4,347
– couple (Category D–over 80)	108.70	5,652	104.60	5,439
Age addition (over 80) (each)	0.25	13	0.25	13
Statutory adoption pay				
Rate[6]	117.18	–	112.75	–
Earnings threshold	90.00	–	87.00	–
Statutory maternity pay				
Rate[6]	117.18	–	112.75	–
Earnings threshold	90.00	–	87.00	–
Statutory paternity pay				
Rate[6]	117.18	–	112.75	–
Earnings threshold	90.00	–	87.00	–
Statutory sick pay				
Rate	75.40	–	72.55	–
Earnings threshold	90.00	–	87.00	–

[1] Paid to widows and widowers for up to 52 weeks.

[2] For weeks 29 to 52. See note below on non-taxable benefits on p 87.

[3] For deaths before 11 April 1988 only.

[4] When paid with retirement pensions. See note below on non-taxable benefits on p 87.

[5] Where the allowance exceeds the amount shown above, the excess is not taxable.

[6] The allowance is 90% of average weekly earnings if less than the above amount. In the first six weeks the rate of SMP is 90% of average weekly earnings even if higher than the standard rate.

Non-taxable state benefits

Weekly rates from	7.4.08	9.4.07
	£	£
Attendance allowance		
Higher rate (day and night)	67.00	64.50
Lower rate (day or night)	44.85	43.15
Child benefit		
Eldest child (before 7.4.08, couple)	18.80	18.10
Each subsequent child	12.55	12.10
Child dependency addition		
Paid with retirement pension, bereavement benefit, carer's allowance, incapacity benefit, higher rate industrial death benefit	11.35	11.35
Disability living allowance		
Care component higher rate	67.00	64.50
middle rate	44.85	43.15
lower rate	17.75	17.10
Mobility component higher rate	46.75	45.00
lower rate	17.75	17.10
Guardian's allowance	13.45	12.95
Incapacity benefit (short-term)[*]		
Under pension age – lower rate (first 28 weeks)	63.75	61.35
– Adult dependency increase	39.40	37.90
Over pension age – lower rate (first 28 weeks)	81.10	78.05
– Adult dependency increase	48.65	46.80
Maternity allowance (where SMP not available)		
Standard rate	117.18	112.75
MA threshold	30.00	30.00
– Adult dependency increase	39.40	37.90
Severe disablement allowance		
Basic rate	51.05	49.15
Age-related addition higher rate	17.75	17.10
middle rate	11.40	11.00
lower rate	5.70	5.50
– Adult dependency increase	30.40	29.25

[*] Incapacity benefit replaced invalidity allowance from April 1995. The benefits are taxable except those paid in the first 28 weeks of incapacity and those paid to persons already receiving invalidity benefit on 13 April 1995 so long as they remain incapable of work.

Other non-taxable benefits include:

Bereavement payment (lump sum £2,000)
Child tax credit (see Tax Credits, p 71)
Christmas bonus (with retirement pension)
Cold weather payments
Council tax benefit (income related)
Earnings top-up
Housing benefit (income related)
Income support (income related)
Industrial death benefit
Industrial injuries disablement pension
Jobfinder's grant
Pension credit (see Tax Credits, p 71)

Pneumoconiosis, byssinosis and miscellaneous disease benefits
Redundancy payment
Social fund payments
Television licence payment
Vaccine damage (lump sum)
War pensions
Winter fuel payment (£200 plus £100 for those aged over 80)
Working tax credit (see Tax Credits, p 71)

Stamp taxes

Stamp duty land tax

Stamp duty land tax applies to contracts entered into (or varied) after 10.7.03 and completed after 30.11.03 and to leases granted after that date. With effect from 22.7.04, it also applies to the transfer of an interest in land into, or out of, a partnership and to the acquisition of an interest in a partnership where the partnership property includes an interest in land. With effect from 19.7.06, it applies to transfers of partnership interests only where the sole or main activity of the partnership is investing or dealing in interests in land.

Land transactions		Consideration[1]	
Effective date	Residential property	Non-residential or mixed property	Rate
From 23.3.06	**Up to £125,000**	**Up to £150,000**	**Nil**
	£125,001–£250,000	**£150,001–£250,000**	**1%**
	£250,001–£500,000	**£250,001–£500,000**	**3%**
	£500,001 or more	**£500,001 or more**	**4%**
17.3.05–22.3.06	Up to £120,000	Up to £150,000	Nil
	£120,001–£250,000	£150,001–£250,000	1%
	£250,001–£500,000	£250,001–£500,000	3%
	£500,001 or more	£500,001 or more	4%
1.12.03–16.3.05	Up to £60,000	Up to £150,000	Nil
	£60,001–£250,000	£150,001–£250,000	1%
	£250,001–£500,000	£250,001–£500,000	3%
	£500,001 or more	£500,001 or more	4%
Lease rentals	On net present value of rent over term of lease (applying a discount rate of 3.5%)[2]		
Effective date	Residential property	Non-residential or mixed property	Rate
From 23.3.06	**Up to £125,000**	**Up to £150,000**	**Nil**
	£125,001 or more	**£150,001 or more**	**1%**
17.3.05–22.3.06	Up to £120,000	Up to £150,000	Nil
	£120,001 or more	£150,001 or more	1%
1.12.03–16.3.05	Up to £60,000	Up to £150,000	Nil
	£60,001 or more	£150,001 or more	1%
Premiums			
The same tax is payable for a premium granted as for a land transaction. Special rules apply to a premium in respect of non-residential property where the rent exceeds £1,000 a year. For transactions before 12 March 2008, the rules applied to all property where the rent exceeded £600 a year.			

[1]   Rates apply to the full consideration, not only to that in excess of the previous band.

[2]   Rates apply to the amount of npv in the slice, not the whole value.

Exemptions and reliefs

No SDLT (or stamp duty) is chargeable on:
(1)   transfers to charities for use for charitable purposes.
(2)   transfers to bodies established for national purposes.
(3)   gifts inter vivos.
(4)   land transfers within groups of companies.
(5)   land transferred in exchange for shares on company reconstruction and acquisitions.
(6)   transfers of intellectual property.
(7)   certain transfers to registered social landlords.
(8)   certain leases granted by registered social landlords.
(9)   transfers of goodwill (after 21.4.02).
(10) sale and leaseback arrangements involving commercial property (after 30.11.03) (extended with effect from 22.7.04 to residential property and lease and leaseback transactions).
(11) certain acquisitions of residential property by house building companies or property traders when people move into a new dwelling or a chain of transactions break down, or by employers involving employee relocations (after 31.11.03) (extended with effect from 22.7.04 for people buying a new home and unable to move into it immediately).
(12) (after 30.11.03 and before 22.3.06) initial acquisition of assets by trustees of a unit trust scheme.
(13) transfers of property to beneficiaries under a will or an intestacy (after 30.11.03).
(14) certain transfers on divorce.
(15) transfers on sale of residential property for a consideration of up to £150,000 in disadvantaged parts of the UK. This also applies to leases broadly, where the relevant rental value does not exceed £150,000 and to premiums unless the annual rent exceeds £600.
(16) from 1.10.06 until 30.9.12 for new zero carbon homes and from 1.10.07 for new zero carbon flats with a purchase price of up to £500,000, there is no SDLT charged. Where the purchase price is in excess of £500,000, the SDLT liability on the purchase price will be reduced by £15,000.

Stamp taxes

For contracts entered into (or varied) after 10 July 2003 and completed after 30 November 2003 and for leases granted after that date, stamp duty is abolished for all transfers other than stocks and marketable securities, and interests in partnerships. From 22 July 2004 stamp duty is also abolished for certain partnership transactions involving an interest in land. From those dates, transfers of land are subject to stamp duty land tax (see p 123).

Transfers of stock and marketable securities		0.5%
Other transfers (including land transactions before the introduction of SDLT)		
On transfer made pursuant to contract after	16.3.99– 27.3.00 9.3.99	28.3.00– 30.11.03 21.3.00
Conveyance or transfer on sale with certificate of value[1]		
Not exceeding £60,000	Nil	Nil
£60,001–£250,000	1.0%	1%
£250,001–£500,000	2.5%	3%
£500,001 or more	3.5%	4%
Conveyance or transfer on sale without certificate of value	3·5%	4%

Lease premiums
The same duty is payable for a premium granted as for a conveyance or transfer on sale (except that special rules apply to a premium where the rent exceeds £600 a year). For instruments executed on or after 12 March 2008, stamp duty is not chargeable where the amount or value of the consideration is less than £1,000.

Lease rentals (before the introduction of SDLT)	
Furnished residential accommodation for definite term of less than one year at rent in excess of £5,000	£5
Leases not exceeding seven years, or for an indefinite term:	
– Up to £5,000 (£500 before 28.3.00) pa	Nil
– Over £5,000 (£500 before 28.3.00) pa	1%
Leases over seven years and up to 35 years	2%
Leases over 35 years and up to 100 years	12%
Leases over 100 years	24%

[1] These rates apply to the full consideration, not only to that in excess of the previous band.

Rounding

Stamp duty is rounded up to the next multiple of £5 in all cases other than for SDRT.

Fixed duties (before the introduction of SDLT)

Leases other than above	£5
Declaration of trust; duplicate or counterpart; exchange or partition; release or renunciation; surrender	£5

Stamp Duty Reserve Tax (SDRT)

Agreements to transfer chargeable securities for money or money's worth (eg renounceable letters of allotment)[1]	0.5%
Chargeable securities put into a clearance service[2] or converted into depositary receipts	1.5%
Dealings of units in unit trusts and shares in open-ended investment companies[3]	0.5%
Transfers of foreign currency bearer shares and agreements to transfer sterling or foreign currency convertible or equity-related loan stock issued by UK companies	0.5%

[1] If the transaction is completed by a duly stamped instrument within six years from the date on which the charge is imposed, the SDRT will be cancelled or repaid.

[2] Where the operator of a clearance service elects to collect and account for SDRT on the normal rate of 0.5% on dealing within the system the higher SDRT charge of 1.5% does not apply.

[3] From 6 April 2001 transfers of units in a unit trust and surrenders of shares in open-ended investment trusts are exempt when held within individual pension accounts.

Interest on unpaid tax

Stamp duty land tax. *From 26 September 2005*: Interest runs from the end of 30 days after the effective date of transaction (normally completion), or the date of a disqualifying event, until the tax is paid. In the case of a deferred payment, interest runs from the date the payment is due until the tax is paid. A penalty carries interest from the date determined until the date of payment.

Stamp duty. *For instruments executed from 1 October 1999*: Interest runs from the end of 30 days after the date the instrument is executed until the tax is paid. Amounts less than £25 are not charged.

Stamp duty reserve tax. Interest is charged from 14 days after the transaction date for exchange transactions and otherwise from seven days after the end of the month of the transaction. Amounts less than £25 are not charged.

Rates: see p 5.

Repayment supplement

Stamp duty land tax. *From 26 September 2005*: Interest is added to repayments of overpaid stamp duty land tax and runs from the date tax was paid or an amount was lodged with HMRC, or the date a penalty was made, to the date the order for repayment is issued.

Stamp duty. *For instruments executed from 1 October 1999*: Interest is added to repayments of overpaid stamp duty and runs from 30 days after the date the instrument is executed or the date of payment if later. Amounts less than £25 are not paid.

Stamp duty reserve tax. Interest is paid from 14 days after the transaction date for exchange transactions and otherwise from seven days after the end of the month of the transaction.

Rates: see p 8.

Penalties

Offence	Penalty
Stamp duty – for instruments executed from 1 October 1999	
Failure to present instrument for stamping within 30 days after execution (or the day in which it is first received in the UK if executed outside the UK) (Stamp Act 1891 s 15B; SI 1999/2537). (Extended to instruments executed from 24 July 2002 for transfers of UK land and buildings, wherever executed (FA 2002 s 114)).	If presented within one year after the end of the 30-day period: the lower of £300 or the amount of the unpaid duty. If presented more than one year after the end of the 30-day period: the greater of £300 or the amount of unpaid duty.
Stamp duty land tax – contracts completed after 30 November 2003	
Failure to deliver a land transaction return by the filing date (FA 2003 Sch 10 paras 3, 4).	£100 if return delivered within three months of filing date, otherwise £200. If not delivered within 12 months, penalty up to amount of tax chargeable.
Failure to comply with notice to deliver return within specified period (FA 2003 Sch 10 para 5).	Up to £60 for each day on which the failure continues after notification.
Fraudulently or negligently delivering an incorrect return or failing to remedy an error without unreasonable delay (FA 2003 Sch 10 para 8).	Up to the difference between the amount payable and the amount that would have been chargeable on the basis of the return delivered.
Fraudulently or negligently giving a self-certificate for a chargeable transaction or failing to remedy an error in respect of such certificate without unreasonable delay (FA 2003 Sch 11 para 3).	Up to the amount of tax chargeable.
Failure to keep and preserve records under FA 2003 Sch 10 para 9 or Sch 11 para 4 (FA 2003 Sch 10 para 11, Sch 11 para 6).	Up to £3,000 unless the information is provided by other documentary evidence.
Failure to comply with notice to produce documents etc under FA 2003 Sch 10 para 14 or Sch 11 para 9 (FA 2003 Sch 10 para 16, Sch 11 para 11).	(a) Initial penalty of £50; (b) further penalty for each day the failure continues up to £30 if penalty determined by HMRC, or £150 if determined by the court.
Failure (from 1 August 2005) to disclose certain SDLT proposals or arrangements (SI 2005/1868; SI 2005/1869).	(a) Initial penalty up to £5,000; (b) further penalty up to £600 per day while failure continues.

Value added tax

Rates

	Rate	VAT fraction
Standard rate	17.5%	7/47
Reduced rate (see p 94)	5.0%	1/21
Flat-rate scheme for farmers	4.0%*	

* Flat rate addition to sale price

Registration limits

UK taxable supplies

A person who makes taxable supplies is liable to be registered:
(*a*) at the end of any month, or
(*b*) at any time, if:

	(a) turnover in the past year[1] (b) turnover in the next 30 days[2] exceeds:	Unless, in the case of (a), turnover for next year not ex- pected to exceed:
1.4.08 onwards	**£67,000**	**£65,000**
1.4.07–31.3.08	£64,000	£62,000
1.4.06–31.3.07	£61,000	£59,000
1.4.05–31.3.06	£60,000	£58,000
1.4.04–31.3.05	£58,000	£56,000
10.4.03–31.3.04	£56,000	£54,000
25.4.02–9.4.03	£55,000	£53,000

[1] The value of taxable supplies in the year then ending.
[2] If there are reasonable grounds for believing the value of taxable supplies will exceed limit.

Supplies from other EC countries ('distance selling')

A business person in another EC country not registered or liable to be registered in the UK is liable to be registered on any day if, in the period beginning with 1 January in that year, the value of supplies by that person to non-taxable persons in the UK exceeds:

1.1.93 onwards	**£70,000**

Acquisitions from other EC countries

A person not registered or liable to be registered under the above rules is liable to be registered:
(*a*) at the end of any month if, in the period beginning with 1 January in that year, the value of taxable goods acquired by that person for business purposes (or for non-business purposes if a public body, charity, club, etc) from suppliers in other EC countries exceeds the following limits; or
(*b*) at any time, if there are reasonable grounds for believing the value of such acquisitions in the next 30 days will exceed the following limits:

1.4.08 onwards	**£67,000**
1.4.07–31.3.08	£64,000
1.4.06–31.3.07	£61,000
1.4.05–31.3.06	£60,000
1.4.04–31.3.05	£58,000
10.4.03–31.3.04	£56,000
25.4.02–9.4.03	£55,000

Deregistration limits

UK taxable supplies

A registered taxable person ceases to be liable to be registered if, at any time, HMRC are satisfied that the value of taxable supplies in the year then beginning will not exceed:

1.4.08 onwards	**£65,000**
1.4.07–31.3.08	£62,000
1.4.06–31.3.07	£59,000
1.4.05–31.3.06	£58,000
1.4.04–31.3.05	£56,000
10.4.03–31.3.04	£54,000
25.4.02–9.4.03	£53,000

Unless the reason for not exceeding the limit during that year is that the person will cease making taxable supplies or suspend making taxable supplies for 30 days or more.

Supplies from other EC countries ('distance selling')

A person registered under these provisions ceases to be liable to be registered if, at any time:
- (a) relevant supplies in year ended 31 December last before that time did not exceed following limit; and
- (b) HMRC are satisfied that value of relevant supplies in year immediately following that year will not exceed following limit:

1.1.93 onwards	**£70,000**

Acquisitions from other EC countries

A person registered under these provisions ceases to be liable to be registered if, at any time:
- (a) relevant acquisitions in year ended 31 December last before that time did not exceed following limits; and
- (b) HMRC are satisfied that value of relevant acquisitions in year immediately following that year will not exceed following limits:

1.4.08 onwards	**£67,000**
1.4.07–31.3.08	£64,000
1.4.06–31.3.07	£61,000
1.4.05–31.3.06	£60,000
1.4.04–31.3.05	£58,000
10.4.03–31.3.04	£56,000
25.4.02–9.4.03	£55,000
1.4.01–24.4.02	£54,000

Annual accounting scheme

A business may, subject to conditions, complete one VAT return a year. Before 1 April 2006, only businesses with taxable turnover up to £150,000 could join the scheme immediately; other businesses had to have been registered for 12 months.

	Can join if taxable supplies in next year not expected to exceed:	Must leave at end of accounting year if taxable supplies exceeded:
1.4.06 onwards	**£1,350,000**	**£1,600,000**
1.4.04–31.3.06	£660,000	£825,000
1.4.01–31.3.04	£600,000	£750,000

Cash accounting scheme

A business may, subject to conditions, account for and pay VAT on the basis of cash paid and received. It can join the scheme at any time as follows.

	Can join if taxable supplies in next year not expected to exceed:	Must leave at end of accounting year if taxable supplies exceed:	Unless turnover for next year not expected to exceed:
1.4.07 onwards	**£1,350,000**	**£1,600,000**	**£1,350,000**
1.4.04–31.3.07	£660,000	£825,000	£660,000
1.4.01–31.3.04	£600,000	£750,000	£600,000

Flat-rate scheme for small businesses

A business which expects its taxable supplies (excluding VAT) in the next year to be no more than £150,000 and its total business income to be no more than £187,500 can opt to join a flat-rate scheme. The appropriate percentage below is applied to total turnover generated, including exempt income, to calculate net VAT due.

Category of business	Appropriate %	
	before 1.1.04	from 1.1.04
Accountancy or book-keeping	13.5	13
Advertising	11	9.5
Agricultural services	9	7.5
Animal husbandry	11	N/A
Any other activity not listed elsewhere	11	10
Architect	13.5	12.5
Boarding or care of animals	N/A	10.5
Business services that are not listed elsewhere	12.5	11
Catering services, including restaurants and takeaways	13	12
Civil and structural engineer or surveyor	N/A	12.5
Computer and IT consultancy or data processing	14.5	13
Computer repair services	13.5	11
Dealing in waste or scrap	11	9.5
Entertainment or journalism	12	11
Estate agency and property management services	11.5	11
Farming or agriculture that is not listed elsewhere	6.5	6
Film, radio, television or video production	N/A	10.5
Financial services	12	11.5
Forestry or fishing	10	9
General building or construction services[1]	9	8.5
Hairdressing or other beauty treatment services	13	12
Hiring or renting goods	9.5	8.5
Hotel or accommodation	10.5	9.5
Labour-only building or construction services[1]	14.5	13.5
Laundry or dry-cleaning services	12	11
Lawyer or legal services	13.5	13
Library, archive, museum or other cultural activity	8.5	7.5
Management consultancy	13.5	12.5
Manufacturing fabricated metal products	11	10
Manufacturing food	8.5	7.5
Manufacturing that is not listed elsewhere	10	8.5
Manufacturing yarn, textiles or clothing	9.5	8.5
Membership organisation	7	5.5
Mining or quarrying	10	9
Packaging	9	8.5
Photography	10	9.5
Post Offices[2] (from 1 April 2004)	N/A	2
Postal and courier services[3] (before 1 April 2004)	6	5.5
Printing	8.5	7.5
Publishing	10	9.5
Pubs	6	5.5
Real estate activity not listed elsewhere	13	12
Repairing personal or household goods	10	8.5
Repairing vehicles	8.5	7.5
Retailing food, confectionery, tobacco, newspapers or children's clothing	5	2
Retailing pharmaceuticals, medical goods, cosmetics or toiletries	8	7
Retailing that is not listed elsewhere	7	6
Retailing vehicles or fuel	8	7
Secretarial services	11.5	11
Social work	9	8.5
Sport or recreation	8	7
Transport or storage, couriers, freight, removals and taxis[3]	10	9
Travel agency	10	9
Veterinary medicine	11	9.5
Wholesaling agricultural products	7	6
Wholesaling food	7	5.5
Wholesaling that is not listed elsewhere	8	7

[1] That is, services where value of materials supplied is less than 10% of turnover of such services; any other services are 'general building or construction services'.

[2] From 1 April 2004 a rate of 2% applies to Post Offices (previously within postal and courier services).

[3] From 1 April 2004 (1 July 2004 for courier businesses applying to join scheme before 3 March 2004) rate for transport is used.

Partial exemption

A registered person who makes taxable and exempt supplies is partly exempt and may not be able to deduct (or reclaim) all his input tax. Where, however, input tax attributable to exempt supplies in a prescribed accounting period or tax year is within the de minimis limits below, all such input tax is attributable to taxable supplies and recoverable (subject to the normal rules).

De minimis limits	£625 per month on average and 50% of all input tax for the period concerned

Capital goods scheme

Input tax adjustment following change in taxable use of capital goods

Item	Value	Adjustment period
Computer equipment	£50,000 or more	Five years
Land and buildings	£250,000 or more	Ten years (five years where interest had less than ten years to run on acquisition)

Adjustment formula

$$\frac{\text{Total input tax on item}}{\text{Length of adjustment period}} \times \text{adjustment percentage}$$

The adjustment percentage is the percentage change in the extent to which the item is used (or treated as used) in making taxable supplies between the first interval in the adjustment period and a subsequent interval. (The first interval generally ends on the last day of the tax year in which the input tax was incurred.)

Zero-rated supplies

A zero-rated supply is a taxable supply, but the rate of tax is nil (VATA 1994 Sch 8).

Group 1 – Food
Group 2 – Sewerage services and water
Group 3 – Books etc
Group 4 – Talking books for the blind and handicapped and wireless sets for the blind
Group 5 – Construction of buildings etc
Group 6 – Protected buildings
Group 7 – International services
Group 8 – Transport

Group 9 – Caravans and houseboats
Group 10 – Gold
Group 11 – Bank notes
Group 12 – Drugs, medicines, aids for the handicapped etc
Group 13 – Imports, exports etc
Group 15 – Charities etc
Group 16 – Clothing and footwear

Reduced rate supplies

(VATA 1994 Sch 7A, SI 2007 No 1601)

Group 1 – Domestic fuel and power
Group 2 – Installation of energy-saving materials
Group 3 – Grant-funded installation of heating equipment or security goods or connection of a gas supply
Group 4 – Women's sanitary products
Group 5 – Children's car seats
Group 6 – Residential conversions
Group 7 – Residential renovations and alterations

Group 8 – Contraceptive products (from 1 July 2006)
Group 9 – Welfare advice or information (from 1 July 2006)
Group 10 – Installation of mobility aids for the elderly (from 1 July 2007)
Group 11 – Smoking cessation products (from 1 July 2007)

Exempt supplies

(VATA 1994 Sch 9)

Group 1 – Land
Group 2 – Insurance
Group 3 – Postal services
Group 4 – Betting, gaming and lotteries
Group 5 – Finance
Group 6 – Education
Group 7 – Health and welfare
Group 8 – Burial and cremation
Group 9 – Subscriptions to trade unions, professional and other public interest bodies

Group 10 – Sport, sports competitions and physical education
Group 11 – Works of art etc
Group 12 – Fund-raising events by charities and other qualifying bodies
Group 13 – Cultural services etc
Group 14 – Supplies of goods where input tax cannot be recovered
Group 15 – Investment gold

Car fuel

VAT-inclusive scale figures are used to assess VAT due on petrol provided at below cost price for private journeys by registered traders or their employees, where the petrol has been provided from business resources. The figures represent the tax-inclusive value of the fuel supplied to each individual and relate to return periods beginning on the dates shown.

	12 months £	VAT due per car £	3 months £	VAT due per car £	1 month £	VAT due per car £
From 1 May 2008: CO_2 band						
120 or below	555	82.66	138	20.55	46	6.85
125	830	123.62	207	30.83	69	10.28
130	830	123.62	207	30.83	69	10.28
135	830	123.62	207	30.83	69	10.28
140	885	131.81	221	32.91	73	10.87
145	940	140.00	234	34.85	78	11.62
150	995	148.19	248	36.94	82	12.21
155	1,050	156.38	262	39.02	87	12.96
160	1,105	164.57	276	41.11	92	13.70
165	1,160	172.77	290	43.19	96	14.30
170	1,215	180.96	303	45.13	101	15.04
175	1,270	189.15	317	47.21	105	15.64
180	1,325	197.34	331	49.30	110	16.38
185	1,380	205.53	345	51.38	115	17.13
190	1,435	213.72	359	53.47	119	17.72
195	1,490	221.91	373	55.55	124	18.47
200	1,545	230.11	386	57.49	128	19.06
205	1,605	239.04	400	59.57	133	19.81
210	1,660	247.23	414	61.66	138	20.55
215	1,715	255.43	428	63.74	142	21.15
220	1,770	263.62	442	65.83	147	21.89
225	1,825	271.81	455	67.77	151	22.49
230	1,880	280.00	469	69.85	156	23.23
235 or above	1,935	288.19	483	71.94	161	23.98
1 May 2007–30 April 2008: CO_2 band						
140 or below	730	108.72	182	27.11	60	8.94
145	780	116.17	195	29.04	65	9.68
150	830	123.62	207	30.83	69	10.28
155	880	131.06	219	32.62	73	10.87
160	925	137.77	231	34.40	77	11.47
165	975	145.21	243	36.19	81	12.06
170	1,025	152.66	256	38.13	85	12.66
175	1,075	160.11	268	39.91	89	13.26
180	1,120	166.81	280	41.70	93	13.85
185	1,170	174.26	292	43.49	97	14.45
190	1,220	181.70	304	45.28	101	15.04
195	1,270	189.15	317	47.21	105	15.64
200	1,315	195.85	329	49.00	109	16.23
205	1,365	203.30	341	50.79	113	16.83
210	1,415	210.74	353	52.57	117	17.43
215	1,465	218.19	365	54.36	121	18.02
220	1,510	224.89	378	56.30	126	18.77
225	1,560	232.34	390	58.09	130	19.36
230	1,610	239.79	402	59.87	134	19.96
235	1,660	247.23	414	61.66	138	20.55
240 or above	1,705	253.94	426	63.45	142	21.15
1 May 2006–30 April 2007						
Diesel engine						
2,000cc or less	1,040	154.89	260	38.72	86	12.81
Over 2,000cc	1,325	197.34	331	49.30	110	16.38
Any other type of engine						
1,400cc or less	1,095	163.09	273	40.66	91	13.55
Over 1,400cc up to 2,000cc	1,385	206.28	346	51.53	115	17.13
Over 2,000cc	2,035	303.09	508	75.66	169	25.17

	12 months £	VAT due per car £	3 months £	VAT due per car £	1 month £	VAT due per car £
1 May 2005–30 April 2006						
Diesel engine						
2,000cc or less	945	140.74	236	35.15	78	11.62
Over 2,000cc	1,200	178.72	300	44.68	100	14.89
Any other type of engine						
1,400cc or less	985	146.70	246	36.64	82	12.21
Over 1,400cc up to 2,000cc	1,245	185.43	311	46.32	103	15.34
Over 2,000cc	1,830	272.55	457	68.06	152	22.64
1 May 2004–30 April 2005						
Diesel engine						
2,000cc or less	865	128.82	216	32.17	72	10.72
Over 2,000cc	1,095	163.08	273	40.65	91	13.55
Any other type of engine						
1,400cc or less	930	138.51	232	34.55	77	11.46
Over 1,400cc up to 2,000cc	1,175	175.00	293	43.63	97	14.44
Over 2,000cc	1,730	257.65	432	64.34	144	21.44
1 May 2003–30 April 2004						
Diesel engine						
2,000cc or less	900	134.04	225	33.51	75	11.17
Over 2,000cc	1,135	169.04	283	42.14	94	14.00
Any other type of engine						
1,400cc or less	950	141.48	237	35.29	79	11.76
Over 1,400cc up to 2,000cc	1,200	178.72	300	44.68	100	14.89
Over 2,000cc	1,770	263.61	442	65.82	147	21.89

Interest and penalties

Default interest

(VATA 1994 s 74)

Interest runs on the amount of any VAT assessed (or paid late by voluntary disclosure):
- from the reckonable date (normally the latest date on which a return is required for the period in question);
- until the date of payment (although in practice it runs to the date shown on the notice of assessment or notice of voluntary disclosure if paid within 30 days of that date).

The period of interest cannot commence more than three years before the date of assessment or payment. The rates of interest are as follows:

Period	Rate
from 6 January 2008	**7.5%**
6 August 2007–5 January 2008	8.5%
6 September 2006–5 August 2007	7.5%
6 September 2005–5 September 2006	6.5%
6 September 2004–5 September 2005	7.5%
6 December 2003–5 September 2004	6.5%
6 August 2003–5 December 2003	5.5%*
6 November 2001–5 August 2003	6.5%
6 May 2001–5 November 2001	7.5%

Interest on VAT overpaid in cases of official error

(VATA 1994 s 78)
Where VAT has been overpaid or underclaimed due to an error by HMRC, then on a claim HMRC must pay interest:

- from the date they receive payment (or authorise a repayment) for the return period in question;
- until the date on which they authorise payment of the amount on which interest is due.

This provision does not require HMRC to pay interest on an amount on which repayment supplement is due. The rates of interest are as follows:

Period	Rate
from 6 January 2008	**4%**
6 August 2007–5 January 2008	5%
6 September 2006–5 August 2007	4%
6 September 2005–5 September 2006	3%
6 September 2004–5 September 2005	4%
6 December 2003–5 September 2004	3%
6 August 2003–5 December 2003	2%*
6 November 2001–5 August 2003	3%
6 May 2001–5 November 2001	4%

* Due to an administrative error the rate of default and statutory interest was too high by one percentage point between 6 August 2003 and 5 September 2003. HMRC will not seek to recover amounts overpaid by HMRC and will seek to identify businesses overcharged (see Business Brief 17/05 as of 9 September 2005).

Repayment supplement – VAT

(VATA 1994 s 79)
Where a person is entitled to a repayment the payment due is increased by a supplement of the greater of:
(xiii)   5% of that amount; or
(xiv)   £50.
The supplement will only be paid if:
  (a)   the return or claim is received by HMRC not later than the last day on which it is required to be made;
  (b)   HMRC do not issue a written instruction making the refund within the relevant period; and
  (c)   the amount shown on the return or claim does not exceed the amount due by more than 5% of that amount or £250, whichever is the greater.
The 'relevant period' is 30 days beginning with the receipt of the return or claim or, if later, the day after the last day of the VAT period to which the return or claim relates.

Penalties and surcharges

Offence	Penalty
Failure to submit return or pay VAT due within time limit (where a return is late but the VAT is paid on time or no VAT is due, a default is recorded but no surcharge arises) (VATA 1994 s 59). Failure to pay tax due under the payment on account scheme on time (VATA 1994 s 59A).	The greater of £30 and a specified percentage of outstanding VAT for period, depending on number of defaults in surcharge period: first default in period 2%, second default 5%, third default 10%, fourth and further defaults 15%. (Surcharge assessments are not issued for sums of less than £200 unless the rate of the surcharge is 10% or more.)
Evasion of VAT: conduct involving dishonesty (VATA 1994 s 60).	Amount of tax evaded or sought to be evaded (subject to mitigation).
Issuing incorrect certificate stating that certain supplies fall to be zero-rated or taxed at the reduced rate (VATA 1994 s 62).	Difference between tax actually charged and tax which should have been charged.
Misdeclaration or neglect (VATA 1994 s 63).	15% of VAT which would have been lost if inaccuracy had not been discovered.
Repeated misdeclarations (VATA 1994 s 64).	15% of VAT which would have been lost if second and subsequent inaccuracies within penalty period had not been discovered.
Material inaccuracy in EC sales statement (VATA 1994 s 65).	£100 for each material inaccuracy in two-year penalty period (which commences following notice of second material inaccuracy).
Failure to submit an EC sales statement (VATA 1994 s 66).	Greater of £50 or a daily penalty (maximum 100 days) £5 for the first, £10 for the second, £15 for the third or subsequent failure in the default period.
Failure to notify liability for registration or a change in nature of supplies by person exempted from registration (VATA 1994 s 67).	Greater of £50 and a specified percentage of the tax for which the person would have been liable, depending on the period of failure: nine months or less 5%; over nine and up to 18 months 10%; over 18 months 15%.
Failure to notify acquisition of excise duty goods or new means of transport (VATA 1994 s 67).	Greater of £50 and: 5% of the tax for which the person would have been liable if period of failure is three months or less, 10% if over three and up to six months and 15% if over six months.
Unauthorised issue of invoices (VATA 1994 s 67).	Greater of £50 and 15% of amount shown as or representing VAT.
Breach of walking possession agreement (VATA 1994 s 68).	50% of VAT due or amount recoverable.

Offence	Penalty
Failure to preserve records for prescribed period.	£500.
Failure to preserve records specified in HMRC direction (VATA 1994 ss 69, 69B).	£200 for each day of failure (maximum 30 days).
Breaches of regulatory provisions, including failure to notify cessation of liability or entitlement to be registered, failure to keep records and non-compliance with any regulations made under VATA 1994 (VATA 1994 s 69).	Greater of £50 and a daily penalty (maximum 100 days) of a specified amount depending on number of failures in preceding two years: £5* per day if no previous failures; £10* per day if one previous failure; £15* per day if two or more previous failures.
Where failure consists of not paying VAT or not making a return in the required time.	*1/6, 1/3 and 1/2 of 1% of the VAT due respectively, if greater.
Breaches of regulatory provisions involving failure to pay VAT or submit return by due date (VATA 1994 s 69).	Greater of £50 and a daily penalty (for no more than 100 days) of a specified amount depending on number of failures in preceding two years: greater of £5 and 1/6% of VAT due if no previous failures; greater of £10 and 1/3% of VAT due if one previous failure; greater of £15 and 1/2% of VAT due if two or more previous failures.
Failure to comply with VAT tribunal directions or summons (VATA 1994 Sch 12 para 10).	Up to £1,000.
Failure to comply with the requirements of the investment gold scheme (FA 2000 s 137).	17.5% of the value of transactions concerned.
Import VAT (FA 2003 ss 24–41):	From 27 November 2003:
– failures relating to non-compliance	maximum penalty of £2,500
– evasion.	maximum penalty equal to VAT sought to be evaded.
Failure to notify the use of a designated avoidance scheme (VATA 1994 Sch 11A paras 10, 11).	15% of the tax avoided (applies to businesses with supplies of £600,000 or more from 1 August 2004).
Failure to disclose certain schemes within 30 days of the due date or the first return affected (VATA 1994 Sch 11A paras 10, 11).	£5,000 (applies to businesses with supplies exceeding £10 million from 1 August 2004).

Penalties under VATA 1994 ss 63 and 64 are to be replaced, and that under VATA 1994 s 60 partially replaced, by a new penalty for careless or deliberate errors in a taxpayer's document under FA 2007 Sch 24 with effect for return periods beginning on or after 1 April 2008 for which the return is required to be made on or after 1 April 2009. Penalties under VATA 1994 s 60 will continue to be charged for acts or omissions not relating to an inaccuracy in a document or failure to notify HMRC of an under-assessment.

Index

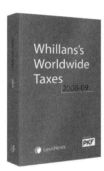